Handbook of English Idioms, Parables and Colloquial Sayings

1001 Sayings With Their Meanings And Sample Usage

By John C. Rigdon

Handbook of English Idioms

1st Printing – Oct 2018 0/0/0/0/kn

Published by:
Eastern Digital Resources
31 Bramblewood Dr. SW
Cartersville, GA 30120
http://www.wordsrus.info
EMAIL: wordsrus@Researchonline.net
Tel. (678) 739-9177

Contents

Introduction

Whether you want to sound more like a native speaker or just know more about the strange expressions you're always hearing, this dictionary is the best way to learn about the English language's most colorful phrases.

This book contains over 1000 commonly encountered English idioms and phrases with an explanation of their meaning and sample usage.

This Dictionary of phrases explores the meanings and origins of terms that may not make literal sense but play an important role in the English language. It is designed to be a reference for those studying English, or anyone who enjoys learning its many wonderful quirks and expressions.

Whether you're looking for cliché's, idioms, jargon, proverbs or colloquial sayings, you'll find them here with an explanation. This edition also features a Thematic Index that cross-references expressions by standard terms and subjects.

We also publish editions of this book with the explanations of the terms in Spanish, French, German, Italian and other languages. Check our website for availability.

Idioms, Proverbs and Colloquial Sayings

1. A **bad excuse is better than none.**

It is better to give a poor or implausible excuse — which may, in fact, be believed — than to have no explanation or justification at all.

2. A **bad penny always turns up.**

Undesirable people will always return; often used when somebody who has left in disgrace reappears after a long absence.

3. A **bad workman always blames his tools.**

Workers who lack skill or competence blame their tools or equipment when things go wrong.
The turkey isn't cooked well because the oven is not functioning well. Well, it's the case of a bad workman blaming his tools.

4. A **barking dog never bites.**

Noisy threats often do not present real danger.

5. A **believer is a songless bird in a cage.**

Religious belief restricts a person's freedom of action and expression.

6. A **bellowing cow soon forgets her calf.**

The loudest laments or complaints are often the first to subside; used specifically of those whose mourning seems excessive.

7. A **bird in the hand is worth two in the bush.**

Something you have for certain now is of more value than better you may get, especially if you risk losing what you have in order to get it.
The question now is will Carmichael live to regret turning down such a lucrative offer? A bird in the hand...

8. A **bleating sheep loses a bite.**

Those who talk too much may miss an important opportunity.

9. A **blind man's wife needs no Paint .**

Attempts to improve the appearance of somebody or something are superfluous when it is the true nature of the person or thing that is of value, or when the improvements will not be appreciated.

10. A **bolt from the blue.**

A sudden, unexpected event
The resignation of the minister this morning came as a bolt from the blue.

11. A **bribe will enter without knocking.**

The use of money enables access where it would otherwise be denied.

12. A **buck .**

Slang term for a the American dollar.

13. A **cat can look at a king.**

Even the lowliest people have the right to look at, or show an interest in, those of higher status or prestige; often used by somebody accused of staring insolently.

14. A **cat has nine lives.**

Cat can survive seemingly fatal events.
I haven't seen him for several weeks, but I wouldn't really worry about him. Everyone knows a cat has nine lives.

15. A **cat in gloves catches no mice.**

It is sometimes necessary to be bold or ruthless, or to do unpleasant things, in order to achieve one's ends.

16. A **cat may look at a king.**

all people have certain minimal rights by virtue of being alive

17. A **chain is only as strong as its weakest link.**

If one member of a team doesn't perform well, the whole team will fail.
No matter how confident the team is, it is as strong as its weakest link – its defence.

18. A **change is as good as a rest.**

Doing something different for a time can be just as refreshing as taking a break from work; also used more generally of any change in routine.

19. A **chip off the old block.**

If you're a chip off the old block, you're similar in some distinct way to your father or mother.
He is as stingy as her mother – a real chip off the old block.

20. A **creaking door hangs longest.**

Those who have many minor ailments and infirmities often outlive those who don't.

21. A **dog is a man's best friend.**

Loyalty and valuable services that dogs provide to human beings make them worthy of being called man's best friend.

22. A **dog that will fetch a bone will carry a bone.**

Beware of people who bring you gossip about others, because they are equally likely to pass on gossip about you.

23. A **dose of adversity is often as needful as a dose of medicine.**

Hardship and misfortune may be unpleasant, but they can sometimes have a beneficial effect on the character, especially when people fail to appreciate the good things they have.

24. A **dripping June sets all in tune.**

A rainy June means there will be a good harvest of crops and flowers later in the summer

25. A **drowning man will clutch at a straw.**

When someone is in a difficult situation, s/he will take any available opportunity to improve it.
After trying all reliable medicines, he is now visiting quacks to get a cure for his baldness. A drowning man will clutch at a straw.

26. A **dwarf on a giant's shoulders sees further of the two.**

Those who build on the breakthroughs of their predecessors surpass their achievements.

27. A **fat kitchen makes a lean will.**

Those who eat well all their lives will have little money left when they die.

28. A fish always rots from the head down.

>A corrupting influence often spreads from a leader to the rest of the organization or group.

29. A fish stinks from the head .

>A corrupting influence often spreads from a leader to the rest of the organization or group.

30. A flash in the pan.

>If you call something flash in the pan, you say it has happened for only one time and it won't repeat.
>*Considering their dismal past record, the win in the last match seems to be a flash in the pan.*

31. A fool and his money are soon parted.

>Foolish people do not know how to hold on to their money.
>*She gave up her entire estate on the basis of a verbal promise. A fool and his money are indeed easily parted.*

32. A fool at forty is a fool indeed.

>People who have not gained the wisdom of experience by the time they reach middle age are likely to remain fools for the rest of their lives

33. A fool may give a wise man counsel.

>People are often able to give good advice to those who are considered to be intellectually superior; sometimes said apologetically by the giver of such advice, or used as a warning against disregarding it.

34. A fool's bolt is soon shot.

>Foolish people act hastily and thus waste their efforts.

35. A **foolish consistency is the hobgoblin of little minds.**

> A lack of flexibility in making judgments is regarded as a sign of petty narrow-mindedness.

36. A **friend in need is a friend indeed.**

> A true friend will stand by you when you are in need.

37. A **golden key can open any door.**

> With money you can gain access to anything you want; used specifically of bribery, or more generally of the power and influence of wealth.

38. A **good beginning makes a good ending.**

> You should try to start well if you expect to end well.

39. A **good dog deserves a good bone.**

> A loyal servant or employee deserves his reward.

40. A **good example is the best sermon..**

> Showing someone something is better than telling them.

41. A **good face is a letter of recommendation.**

> An honest demeanor may be interpreted as a sign of a person's integrity.

42. A **good horse cannot be of a bad color .**

> Superficial appearances do not affect the essential worth of something.

43. A **good husband makes a good wife..**

People who live or work together should set a good example to each other — a good husband will have a good wife, a good master will have a good servant, and so on.

44. A **good Jack makes a good Jill.**

People who live or work together should set a good example to each other — a good husband will have a good wife, a good master will have a good servant, and so on.

45. A **good man is hard to find.**

A proverb, bemoaning the difficulty of finding a suitable male partner.

46. A **good name is better than precious ointment.**

Your good name should be your most cherished possession.

47. A **good reputation is more valuable than money..**

Your good name should be your most cherished possession.

48. A **good tale is not the worse for being told twice.**

There is no harm in telling a good joke or anecdote — or a story with a moral — a second time; often used by way of apology or justification for such repetition.

49. A **goose quill is more dangerous than a lion's claw.**

Written words of criticism or defamation can do more harm or cause more pain than a physical attack.

50. A **great book is a great evil.**

A long book is a bad book — good writers know how to express themselves concisely.

51. A **great city, a great solitude.**

People often feel more lonely in a large city, among thousands of strangers, than they would do if they were actually alone.

52. A **growing youth has a wolf in his stomach.**

Adolescent boys are perpetually hungry.

53. A **heavy purse makes a light heart.**

Those who have plenty of money are happy and carefree.

54. A **hedge between keeps friendship green..**

A good relationship between neighbors depends on each respecting the other's privacy and not entering his or her property uninvited; also used more broadly of international relations and the need to maintain trade barriers and border controls.

55. A **horse can't pull while kicking.**

People engaged in acts of insubordination or protest cannot work efficiently or productively.

56. A **house divided against itself cannot stand.**

an endeavor that is at cross-purposes with itself will fall. *Bible Reference: Matthew 12:22*

57. A **house is not a home.**

Love is needed to make a house a home.
A chair is still a chair. Even when there's no one sitting there. But a chair is not a house. And a house is not a home. When there's no one there to hold you tight

58. A house without books is like a room without windows.

Books brighten and enlighten our daily lives in the same way that windows brighten and illuminate a room.

59. A hungry stomach has no ears.

There is no point in talking to or reasoning with hungry people, or those who are greedily devouring their food.

60. A jack of all trades is master of none.

Somebody who has a very wide range of abilities or skills usually does not excel at any of them.

61. A jackass can kick a barn door down, but it takes a carpenter to build one.

Something that has taken time, skill, and effort to put together can be quickly ruined or destroyed by a foolish person.

62. A journey of a thousand miles begins with a single step.

Howsoever big a task is, it starts with a small step.
I'm feeling overwhelmed by the prospect of completing my 4,000-word paper by next week, but I guess I'll start by writing 500 words every day. After all, a journey of a thousand miles begins with a single step.

63. A leopard cannot change its spots.

A thing is as it appears. It cannot change.

64. A liar is worse than a thief.

People who lie are even less trustworthy than people who thieve.

65. A lie can go around the world and back again while the truth

is lacing up its boots.

> False rumors travel with alarming speed.

66. **A little absence does much good.**

> A short period of absence can have a surprisingly beneficial effect.

67. **A little knowledge is a dangerous thing.**

> A small amount of knowledge can mislead people into thinking that they are more expert than they really are.

68. **A little pot is soon hot.**

> Small people are reputed to be more easily angered than others.

69. **A man can only die once.**

> Death can only happen once in a lifetime.

70. **A man is a lion in his own cause.**

> People tend to exceed expectations when they have a personal interest in something.

71. **A man who is his own lawyer has a fool for his client.**

> It is not wise to act as your own attorney in a court of law, or in some other legal process; also used in other fields of activity requiring professional expertise or objectivity.

72. **A man wrapped up in himself makes a very small bundle.**

> Self-centeredness is not a quality that is associated with greatness.

73. **A man's got to do what a man's got to do.**

You must do what needs to be done, or what you feel ought to be done, however unpleasant it may be; sometimes used facetiously.

74. A **man's home is his castle.**

People have the right to privacy and freedom of action in their own home.

75. A **man's word is as good as his bond.** .

Honorable people do not break their promises

76. A **mind is a terrible thing to waste.** .

Everybody should make best use of the intellectual capacity they have

77. A **miss is as good as a mile.** .

If you fail, the margin of failure is irrelevant

78. A **penny saved is a penny earned.**

Save your money. Saving money is just like making money.

79. A **picture is worth a thousand words.**

An image can tell a story better than words
"I wasn't sure that he loved her, but then I saw them hugging at the airport. A picture is worth a thousand words."

80. A **piece of cake.**

If something is a piece of cake, it's easy to do.
Solving such math problems is a piece of cake for me.

81. A **rich man's joke is always funny.**

Wealthy people never lack friends — or those who claim to be their friends until their money runs out.

82. A **rolling stone gathers no moss.**

A person who is always changing jobs and places has the advantage of less responsibilities, but also the disadvantage of no fixed place to live.
He was a bit of rolling stone before he got the job and settled down.

83. A **ship in the harbor is safe, but that is not what a ship is for.**

Get out of your comfort zone to grow and fulfill your potential.
I think your fears are unfounded. You should travel to Italy for the Model UN. I'm sure you'll learn a lot. Remember, a ship in the harbor is safe, but that is not what a ship is for.

84. A **shot in the dark.**

A wild guess
Chasing an offender, the policemen took a shot in the dark and turned left on reaching the square.

85. A **stitch in time saves nine.**

It's better to deal with problems immediately rather than wait by when they worsen and become much bigger.
Because we anticipated and responded to the possible change in Facebook algorithm, the referral traffic to our website dropped much less than what happened to some of our competitors. A stitch in time saves nine.

86. A **thing begun is half done.**

A good beginning makes it easier to accomplish the rest of the project.
He has already won first set in the match. I think he is on course to take this match. Well begun is half done, after all.

87. A **thing of beauty is a joy forever..**

The memory of something beautiful remains long after the beauty is faded.

88. A **watched pot never boils.**

If something takes time to do, it doesn't help to constantly check on it. You just have to give it time.
"I know you think he's going to be a great guitar player one day, but stop criticizing him so much. He just started taking lessons two weeks ago! A watched pot never boils."

89. **Absence is the mother of disillusion.**

A period of separation may enable you to consider people or things more objectively and see them in a truer but less favorable light

90. **Absence makes the heart grow fonder.**

Being away from someone or something for a period of time makes you appreciate that person or thing more when you see them or it again
"I used to hate going to my aunt's house, but now I kind of miss it. Absence makes the heart grow fonder."

91. **Accidents will happen in the best-regulated families.**

No matter how careful you are, you may still do something by accident or mistake; often used to console somebody who has done such a thing.

92. **Accusing the times is but excusing ourselves.**

People who seek to blame the times or conditions they live in are really trying to avoid taking the blame themselves

93. **Ace up one's sleeve.**

A secret or hidden advantage that you can use when you need it
Murali, the mystery bowler whom the opposite team has never played, is an ace up the home team's sleeve.

94. Ace .

Positive exclamation, equivalent to 'great!' or 'Awesome!'

95. Actions speak louder than words.

Actions are a better reflection of one's character because it's easy to say things, but difficult to act on them and follow through.
Julie always says she'll donate to the school, and she never does, so I doubt she will this year. Actions speak louder than words, after all.

96. Admiration is the daughter of ignorance.

People often admire others about whom they only have incomplete knowledge

97. Adventures are to the adventurous.

Those who are not bold, and who take no risks, will not have exciting lives or achieve spectacular things

98. Adversity makes strange bedfellows.

In times of hardship or misfortune people often befriend or form alliances with those whose company they would normally avoid

99. Against the clock.

If you're working against the clock, you're working in great hurry.
With only half the syllabus studied, I raced against the clock to be ready for the exam on Monday.

100. Agree, for the law is costly.

> It is expensive to settle disputes in court because of the legal costs involved.

101. Alcohol will preserve anything but a secret.

> People have a tendency to talk too freely and become indiscreet when they are drunk.

102. All animals are equal, but some are more equal than others..

> No person is born superior or inferior to another, so all should have equal rights.

103. All arts are brothers, each is a light to the other.

> The arts should not be considered as separate entities but as parts of one whole, each complementing and leading to a better understanding and appreciation of the others.

104. All cats are gray in the dark.

> People have no distinguishing features, and their appearance becomes unimportant, in the dark; sometimes used with reference to a person's choice of sexual partner

105. All fish are not caught with flies.

> In some circumstances different methods must be employed to achieve a desired end.

106. All good things must come to an end.

> Good experiences eventually come to an end.
> *I was so sad to graduate from college and leave all of my friends, but I've to realize that all good things come to an end.*

107. All is fish that comes to the net.

Everything, no matter how small or unpromising, can be put to use

108. All is grist that comes to the mill..

Everything, no matter how small or unpromising, can be put to use

109. All men are created equal.

No person is born superior or inferior to another, so all should have equal rights.

110. All roads lead to Rome.

There are many different routes to the same goal.
Mary was criticizing the way Jane was planting the flowers. John said, "Never mind, Mary, all roads lead to Rome." Some people learn by doing. Others have to be taught. In the long run, all roads lead to Rome.

111. All that glitters is not gold.

Things that look good outwardly may not be as valuable or good.
I want to be a movie star when I grow up. Film industry looks good from the distance, but it has its own problems. Remember, all that glitters is not gold.

112. All things are possible with God.

Nothing is impossible to the divine will; often used more generally to imply that anything might happen.

113. All words are pegs to hang ideas on.

Words are simply tools for the formulation and communication of ideas.

114. All work and no play makes Jack a dull boy.

People who do not make time for leisure activities risk damaging their health, the quality of their work, or their personal relationships; often used to justify a break from work or to persuade somebody to take one.

115. All's fair in love and war.

One can break the rules of fair play under extenuating circumstances.
How can you pitch my idea to the boss to look good? Come on, all is fair in love and war.

116. All's for the best in the best of all possible worlds.

Everything that happens does so for a good reason, and things in general cannot be any better; generally used to present an optimistic worldview.

117. All's well that ends well.

As long as the outcome is good, problems on the way don't matter.
I'm glad you finally got here, even though your car had a flat tire on the way. Oh well, all's well that ends well.

118. Allow the dust to settle.

To allow a situation to become calm or normal again after a period of excitement or upheaval
Farmers are angry because of the low prices at which government agencies are buying their produce. Let's wait for the dust to settle before we negotiate with them.

119. Alright?.

This is a greeting, comprising 'all right', as in; 'is all right with you?'. It is usually said as a question. An acceptable response would be to mimic the greeting; 'Alright mate' *'Alright'*.

120. Always in a hurry, always behind.

When you try to do things too quickly you work less efficiently and ultimately take longer.

121. Always put your best foot forward.

Try as hard as you can or give your best.
You need to put your best foot forward in the interview if you want to land that job.

122. Always something new out of Africa.

Africa is an endless source of novelty and interest.

123. Among the blind the one-eyed man is king.

An incapable person can gain powerful position if others in the fray are even more incapable.
Despite his obvious lack of exposure and skills, he became head of the department because he is one-eyed among the blind.

124. An ape's an ape, a varlet's a varlet, though they be clad in silk or scarlet.

The true nature of a person or thing may be hidden by outside appearance but cannot be changed.

125. An apple a day keeps the doctor away.

Eating an apple a day will keep you healthy.
Switch from chips to apples for your snack. An apple a day keeps the doctor away.

126. An arm and a leg.

If something costs an arm and a leg, it costs a lot.
Two days in the hospital for a minor ailment cost me an arm and a leg.

127. An army marches on its stomach.

You must eat well if you want to work effectively or achieve great things.

128. An empty sack cannot stand upright.

People who are poor or hungry cannot survive, work effectively, or remain honest.

129. An empty vessel makes much noise.

Foolish or stupid people are the most talkative.
The spokesperson of the ruling political party yesterday was shouting at the top of his voice on a TV debate, trying to defend the indefensible. Empty vessel makes much noise.

130. An eye for an eye and a tooth for a tooth.

If someone does something wrong, then they should be punished by same degree of injury or punishment.
I won't be satisfied with such paltry punishment to the wrongdoers. An eye for an eye, a tooth for a tooth; this I demand from all who have wronged me.

131. An hour in the morning is worth two in the evening.

People are at their most efficient early in the day, when they are refreshed by sleep.

132. An idle brain is the devil's workshop.

If you've nothing to do, you'll likely think of mischief.
The kids should be kept busy during the summer break. Otherwise, you know an idle brain is devil's workshop.

133. An ounce of protection is worth a pound of cure.

A little precaution before a crisis hits is better than lot of firefighting afterwards.

23

Get the vaccination on priority. An ounce of protection is worth a pound of cure.

134. Another day, another dollar.

However hard or tedious paid work may be, at least there is some financial reward; often said with relief at the end of the working day or, more generally, in the hope of a better day tomorrow.

135. Any port in a storm.

In desperate circumstances people will accept help from any source, including those they would normally shun.

136. Any publicity is good publicity.

Even bad publicity draws attention to a person or product and may therefore serve a useful purpose.

137. Appearances are deceiving; judge not according to appearances..

Superficial appearances do not affect the essential worth of something.

138. Appetite comes with eating.

Desire or enthusiasm for something often increases as you do it

139. April showers bring May flowers.

Something unpleasant often leads to something more desirable.

140. As a tree falls, so shall it lie.

People should not attempt to change their beliefs or opinions just because they are about to die.

141. As **fit as a fiddle.**

To be very healthy and strong.
The deputy Prime Minister is 87, but he's as fit as a fiddle.

142. As **good be an addled egg as an idle bird.**

Somebody who tries and fails has achieved no less than somebody who does nothing at all; used as a reprimand for idleness or inaction.

143. As **Maine goes, so goes the nation.**

The members of a large group will follow the lead of an infl uential part of the group.

144. As **the day lengthens, so the cold strengthens.**

The coldest part of the winter often occurs in the period following the shortest day, as the hours of daylight begin to grow longer.

145. As **the twig is bent, so is the tree inclined.**

A child's early education and training are of great importance in determining the way he or she will grow up.

146. As **you make your bed, so you must lie in it.**

You must put up with the unpleasant results of a foolish action or decision.

147. As **you sow, so you shall reap.**

Your actions – good or bad – determine what you get.
You've got entangled in few cases of fraud. That's a result of your illegal get-rich-quick methods. You should have known as you sow, so you shall reap.

148. Ask me no questions and I'll tell you no lies.

It is better not to ask questions that somebody is likely to be unwilling to answer truthfully; used in response to such a question or simply to discourage an inquisitive person.

149. Away goes the devil when he finds the door shut against him.

Evil will never triumph if all temptations are rejected.

150. Aye .

It means yes. It is commonly used in Scotland. It was used in the film "Brave Heart",

151. Back against the wall.

Be in a difficult situation from where escape is difficult
Example: With banks baying for his blood over default in payments, he has his back against the wall.

152. Back the wrong horse.

To support a person or action that later turns out to be unsuccessful
The political party fielded a businessman from the prestigious seat in the national capital, but he lost.They clearly backed the wrong horse.

153. Back to the drawing board.

If you go back to the drawing board, you make a fresh start or try another idea because the earlier one didn't succeed.
After the new product failed to set the sales number rolling, the team went back to the drawing board.

154. Bad money drives out good.

The existence or availability of something inferior or worthless — whether it be money, music, literature, or whatever — has a tendency to make things of better quality or greater value more scarce.

155. Bail.

Intransitive verb for leaving abruptly.

156. Ball and Chain .

A wife or female spouse. Referring to the ball and chain attached to the ankles of prisoners in times gone by.

157. Ballistic .

From the original meaning of a type of missile, in slang this describes a fit of anger and rage.

158. Balls up .

A mistake leading to a negative outcome, equal to 'messed up'.

159. Barking dogs seldom bite.

People who appear threatening rarely can do harm.
I'm really scared to report the delay in the project to the boss. His temper is so over the top. I don't think you should worry too much about it. Barking dogs seldom bite.

160. Barking up the wrong tree.

To ask the wrong person or follow the wrong course
The sales team blamed the engineers for the organization's failure to bag the mega deal, but they were barking up the wrong tree.

161. Barmy .

Crazy or insane.

162. **Barry .**

Another term from the Scots, meaning 'good' when
exclaimed, or at least 'okay'

163. **Be in a tight spot.**

To be in a difficult situation
*If the government fails to get support from its key ally, it'll be in
a tight spot during the voting tomorrow.*

164. **Be just before you're generous.**

You should make sure all your debts are paid and other
obligations met before you start giving money away or
living extravagantly.

165. **Be off the mark.**

If something is off the mark, it is incorrect or inaccurate.
*The meteorology department was quite off the mark in predicting
rainfall this week.*

166. **Be the day weary or be the day long, at last it ringeth to
evensong.**

No matter how tiring or stressful a day you are
having,you can console yourself with the fact that it will
eventually be over; also used more generally to
recommend perseverance or endurance in a trying
situation.

167. **Bear and forbear.**

Patience, tolerance,endurance, and forgiveness are
valuable qualities in all walks of life.

168. **Beastly .**

Nasty, unpleasant, particularly when describing somebodies behavior.

169. Beat a retreat.

If you beat a retreat, you withdraw from a dangerous or unpleasant situation.
Seeing the cops, the arsonists beat a hasty retreat.

170. Beauty draws with a single hair.

A beautiful woman has great powers of attraction.

171. Beauty is a good letter of introduction.

Beautiful people make a better first impression on strangers than ugly people do.

172. Beauty is but a blossom.

Good looks do not last.

173. Beauty is in the eye of the beholder.

What may seem beautiful to one person may not seem to another.
You may not like the curves of my new car, but then beauty is in the eye of the beholder.

174. Beauty is only skin deep.

A person's character, intellect, and other inner qualities are more important than his/ her physical beauty.
That gorgeous actress behaved so rudely with the driver – beauty is skin deep, after all.

175. Beauty is truth, truth beauty.

The qualities of beauty and truth are, or should be, inseparable and interlinked;often used when real life falls short of this ideal

176. Beef .

Disagreement or physical aggression between people.

177. Beggar Off .

Meaning 'go away', an old fashioned term that originated from evicting someone out of your house and effectively telling them to go and beg.

178. Beggars can't be choosers.

People who depend on the generosity of others can't pick & choose things as per their liking.They've to accept what is given to them.
I borrowed this jacket from my friend, but it's not one of his nice ones. Well, but, beggars can't be choosers.

179. Behind one's back.

If you do something behind someone's back, you do it secretly without their knowledge (used in negative way).
I don't give a damn to people who say all sorts of things behind my back.

180. Believing has a core of unbelieving.

Belief and unbelief are closely related, and sometimes you need to start from a position of skepticism to arrive at the truth.

181. Bell the cat.

To undertake a risky or dangerous task
Who's going to bell the cat and tell the teacher that no one else but her son has pulled off the mischief?

182. Bend over backwards.

To try please or accommodate someone to an unusual degree
The hotel staff bent over backwards to make the visit of the dignitaries a memorable one.

183. Better a big fish in a little pond than a little fish in a big pond.

It is better to have a position of importance in a small organization than to be an unimportant member of a large group.

184. Better a dinner of herbs where love is than a stalled ox where hate is.

It is better to be poor or dine badly in a loving environment than to eat well or have a wealthy lifestyle in an atmosphere of discord or hatred.

185. Better a good cow than a cow of a good .

A person's character is of more importance than his or her family background.

186. Better a little fire to warm us than a big one to burn us.

Sometimes it is more desirable to have only a small amount of something.

187. Better be the head of a dog than the tail of a lion..

It is better to have a position of importance in a small organization than to be an unimportant member of a large group.

188. Better late than never.

It is better to get something (you desire) late than get it never.
I'm sorry I'm late to the party, but better late than never, right?

189. Better one house spoiled than two.

It is a good thing for two bad, foolish, or otherwise undesirable people to become husband and wife and thus avoid causing trouble in two separate marriages.

190. Better the devil you know than the devil you don't know.

It is often preferable to choose or stay with people or things you know, despite their faults, than to risk replacing them with somebody or something new but possibly less desirable.

191. Better to be poor and healthy rather than rich and sick.

Good health is more important than money.
The pharma tycoon has been in and out of hospital for the last two months because of kidney ailments. It's better to be poor and healthy than rich and sick.

192. Between the devil and the deep blue sea.

If you're caught between the devil and the deep blue sea, you're caught between two undesirable alternatives.
If you support your son, your business partner will be hurt, and vice versa. You're caught between the devil and the deep blue sea.

193. Beware of an oak, it draws the stroke;avoid an ash, it counts the flash; creep under the thorn, it can save you from harm.

It is dangerous to shelter from lightning under the oak, ash, or other trees.

194. Beware of Greeks bearing gifts.

It is wise to be suspicious of offers or friendly gestures made by enemies or opponents.

195. Birds of a feather flock together.

People who are similar spend time together
*"I think we all started hanging out because we all liked anime.
Birds of a feather flock together."*

196. Birth is much but breeding more.

A person's upbringing counts for more in the long run
than the traits of character he or she was born with.

197. Bite off more than you can chew.

To try to do something that is too difficult for you
*He has taken more responsibilities as he couldn't say 'no' to his
boss. I think he has bitten more than he can chew, and he'll
struggle to handle them all.*

198. Bite the Bullet .

When you decide to do something difficult or unpleasant
that one has been putting off or hesitating over.

199. Bitter pill to swallow.

Something such as failure or rejection that is difficult to
accept, but has to be accepted
*Not getting admission to any of the colleges I applied to is a
bitter pill to swallow.*

200. Bladdered .

Extremely drunk.

201. Blessings brighten as they take their flight.

People often fail to appreciate the good things that they
have until they lose them.

202. Blinding .

Too a great extent. 'It was a blinding performance' = 'It was a great performance'.

203. Blinkered .

Having a narrow minded attitude or limited view on something.

204. Bloke .

Nickname for a male, usually used by males.

205. Blood is thicker than water.

Relationships with family (or blood relatives) is stronger than other relationships.
My friends invited me for the picnic on Sunday, but I have to go to my cousin's birthday instead. Blood is thicker than water, isn't it?

206. Blood will have blood.

One act of violence provokes another, by way of revenge blood will tell Inherited characteristics — whether good or bad — cannot be hidden forever.

207. Bloody .

A very old swear word, one that has become so familiar it is considered more fun than offensive.

208. Blooming/Bleeding .

A negative adjective, similar to 'Bloody'

209. Blow hot and cold.

If you blow hot and cold, you vacillate.
Example: The editor blew hot and cold over the story for few days and then finally decided to publish it.

210. Blow someone's cover.

To reveal someone's secret identity and what they're doing
The police blew the cover on the plot by tapping kidnappers' phones.

211. Blow your own trumpet.

If you blow your own trumpet, you tell people how good or successful you are (used in negative way).
That doctor can be so off-putting. He is always blowing his trumpet mentioning his awards and positions in various associations.

212. Boil the ocean.

If you try to boil the ocean, you try to accomplish something too ambitious.
You expect our plant to manufacture 40,000 parts in a week. You're trying to boil the ocean on this one.

213. Bollocks .

Male reproductive organs, but usually used to describe something as 'rubbish' or 'no good'.

214. Bought the farm.

"I didn't know he wanted to move to the country," is how a British person might respond to hearing this phrase. At this point 'bought the farm,' is a general reference to untimely death. However, the phrase originates from WWII-era military accidents involving unreliable aircraft crashing into rural European countryside properties resulting in damages for which the U.S. Government was responsible to pay, thereby, 'buying the farm,' so to speak.

215. Bounce something off someone.

If you bounce something off someone, you discuss ideas or plan with someone to get their view on it.
Can I see you after the office to bounce few ideas off you? Sure. Let's meet at 6 PM.

216. Boys will be boys.

Boys must be forgiven for their bad or boisterous behavior; also used ironically when grown men behave in an irresponsible or childish manner.

217. Bravo .

Well done, or congratulations.

218. Break fresh/ new ground.

If you break new ground, you do something that was not done before.
Our scientists are breaking new ground in robotics and cancer research.

219. Break the Ice .

To initiate social interchanges and conversation; to get something started.

220. Bugger all .

Very little, almost nothing or completely nothing.

221. Burn not your house to scare away the mice.

Do not try to solve a minor problem by taking action that will cause much greater harm.

222. Burn the candle at both ends.

If you burn the candle at both ends, you work excessively hard, say, by keeping two jobs or by leading a busy social life in the evening.
Mitch is burning the candle at both ends. He is working two jobs, one in the evening.

223. Burn the midnight oil.

To work late in the night
I had to burn the midnight oil for nearly three months to write my first book.

224. Burn your boats/ bridges.

If you burn your boats, you do something that makes it impossible to change your plans and go back to the earlier position or situation.
I've burnt my boats with my previous supervisor by criticizing him publicly.

225. Busy folks are always meddling.

It is in the nature of busy people to interfere in the affairs of others.

226. By the skin of your teeth.

By extremely narrow margin
He caught the train by the skin of his teeth.

227. Caesar's wife must be above suspicion.

Those in positions of importance — and their associates — must lead blameless lives and have spotless reputations.

228. Calamity is the touchstone of a brave mind.

It is at times of crisis that you find out who the truly strong, courageous, or great people are.

229. Call a man a thief and he will steal.

Give a person a bad reputation and he or she may start to justify it.

230. Call a spade a spade.

To speak truth even if it's unpleasant
He doesn't hold his words and calls a spade a spade.

231. Call it a day.

If you call it a day, you stop what you're doing because you're tired of it or you've not been successful.
Faced with increasing competition and thinning profits, the owner decided to call it a day after twenty years in the business.

232. Call the shots.

If you calls the shots, you have the power and authority.
In this ministry, the junior minister calls the shots.

233. Can't make heads or tails of something.

Can't understand someone or something at all
I haven't been able to make head or tale of the bugs in the software so far.

234. Care is no cure.

Worrying about something does nothing to put it right.

235. Cast pearls before swine.

If you cast pearls before swine, you offer something valuable to someone who does not recognize its worth.
Example: To serve an elaborate multi-course dinner to them is like casting pearls before swine.

236. Catch not at the shadow and lose the substance.

Do not allow yourself to be distracted from your main purpose by irrelevancies.

237. Catching's before hanging.

Offenders can only be punished when or if they are caught.

238. Chalk and Cheese .

Two things that do not go together, or go together very badly.

239. Change hands.

If something changes hands, it gets a new owner.
This car has changed hands so many time since its first buy in 2009.

240. Change tune.

If you change your tune, you change the way you behave with others from good to bad.
After he came to know that I'm close to the power in the organization, he changed his tune.

241. Chap .

A man, particularly of gentlemanly nature.

242. Charity is not a bone you throw to a dog but a bone you share with a dog.

There should be more to charity than simply giving money or other material goods — it is better to establish a relationship with those in need and to work with them for the benefit of all concerned.

243. Chat up .

Speaking flirtatiously, or speaking to someone with the intention of expressing affection.

244. Cheers .

Expressing good wishes with a drink, traditionally glasses are knocked together while 'cheers' is exclaimed and then a drink is taken. Cheers can also be used generally to replace thanks and as a sign off from a conversation.

245. Chicken and egg situation.

If a situation is chicken and egg, it is impossible to decide which of the two came first and caused the other one.
I need to have experience to get job, but without job, I can't have experience. It's a chicken and egg situation.

246. Children and fools speak the truth.

Children and foolish people have a tendency to say what is true, because they have not learned that it may be advantageous or diplomatic to do otherwise.

247. Children are certain cares, but uncertain comforts.

Children are bound to cause their parents anxiety, and may or may not also bring them joy.

248. Christmas comes but once a year.

Extravagance and self-indulgence at Christmas — or any other annual celebration — can be justified by the fact that it is a relatively infrequent occurrence.

249. Circumstances alter cases.

The same general principle cannot be applied to every individual case, and what is right, good, or appropriate in one set of circumstances may be wrong in another.

250. Cleanliness is next to godliness.

Be clean. God likes that.

251. Cleanliness is next to godliness.

It's good to be clean. God is clean, and you should be too. *"Go take a shower before your date. You know what they say; cleanliness is next to godliness."*

252. Clear the decks.

If you clear the decks for something, you remove all hurdles to get started on that work.
By sanctioning the budget and filling in the vacancies, the committee has cleared the decks for our new office.

253. Close the door on someone.

If you close the door on someone or something, you no longer deal with it.
The country decided to close the door on talks till other outstanding issues are resolved.

254. Clothes do not make the man.

A person's character can't be judged by his/ her clothing and outward appearance.
I can't believe he has been charged for insider trading. He always seemed so professional and impeccable. Well, clothes don't make the man.

255. Clothes make the man..

People are impressed by someone who is well dressed.

256. Cock up .

A badly executed plan or a mistake.

257. Coming events cast their shadows before.

Future events, especially those of some significance, can often be predicted from the warning signs that precede them.

258. Common fame is seldom to blame.

Rumors are rarely without substance, and if unpleasant things are being said about somebody, then that person has probably done something to deserve them.

259. Confess and be hanged.

There is little incentive for confession when punishment is the inevitable result; used as justification for not owning up to wrongdoing.

260. Conscience gets a lot of credit that belongs to cold feet .

Something commended as an act of conscience may be simply due to cowardice or loss of nerve.

261. Cool your heels.

Wait for something, especially when it's annoying
I spent two hours cooling my heels in the waiting room while the CFO was busy in a meeting.

262. Couch Potato.

A lazy person who spends the bulk of their time engaged in things that can be done while sitting on a couch.

263. Councils of war never fight.

When a number of people get together to discuss something important, they rarely decide on a drastic course of action.

264. Courage is fear that has said its prayers.

A brave person is not necessarily fearless, but has drawn strength from religion or some other source.

265. Courtesy is contagious.

If you are polite to other people, then they will be polite to you.

266. Cowards die many times before their deaths.

Cowards suffer the feared effects of death many times over in their lives.
He is constantly worried about the security of his job, and I don't think he'll pursue his true interests. He exemplifies the saying 'cowards die many times before their deaths'.

267. Crack On .

To get on with something, or continue doing something.

268. Cracking .

A positive exclamation or describing something as good.

269. Cram.

To study feverishly before an exam typically done after neglecting to study consistently.

270. Crash.

To abruptly fall asleep, or to show up without invitation.

271. Cream always comes to the top.

People of great worth or quality will ultimately enjoy high achievement or public recognition.

272. Creep (n.

An unpleasantly weird/strange person.

273. Crikey .

A neutral exclamation

274. Crime doesn't pay.

Criminal activity may seem to be profitable, at least in the short term, but it ultimately leads to far greater loss — of liberty, or even of life;used as a deterrent slogan.

275. Crime must be concealed by crime.

One crime often leads to another, committed to avoid detection of the first.

276. Cross the stream where it is shallowest.

To do things in the easiest possible way.
Let's just cross the stream where it is shallowest and find a spot that you can pull right in to — don't worry about parallel parking.

277. Crosses are ladders that lead to heaven.

Suffering and misfortune often bring out the best in a person's character.

278. Cry for the moon.

If you cry for the moon, you make a demand that can't be fulfilled.
You want such an expensive gift on your birthday. Well, you're crying for the moon.

279. Curiosity killed the cat.

Enquiring into others' work can be dangerous. One should mind own business.
I know curiosity killed the cat, but I can't stop the investigation until I know where the donations are really going.

280. Curses, like chickens, come home to roost.

Wrongdoers ultimately have to suffer the consequences of their bad deeds;also used when those who have wished evil on others are struck by misfortune themselves.

281. Cut corners.

If you cut corners, you save money or effort by finding cheaper or easier ways to do things.
It you cut corners on this product, it'll have a lesser lifespan.

282. Cut no ice.

Fail to influence or make an effect
His reason to get leave cut no ice with his manager.

283. Cut someone down to size.

If you cut someone down to size, you show them they're not as important or intelligent as they think.
The boss cut that arrogant guy to size in no time.

284. Cut your coat according to your cloth.

Match your actions to your resources, and do not try to live beyond your means.

285. Daft .

More affectionate today than it was in the past, meaning silly behavior, at worst; stupid.

286. **Dapper** .

Well dressed and/or well to-do.

287. **Daylight robbery.**

Blatant overcharging
$5 for a can of juice! This is daylight robbery.

288. **Dead men don't bite.**

A dead person can no longer do others any harm; often used to justify murder.

289. **Dead men tell no tales.**

It may be expedient to kill somebody who could betray a secret or give information about the criminal activities of others.

290. **Dear** .

Dear can mean expensive, but is more commonly a term of endearment, particularly for women or spouses.

291. **Death is the great leveler.**

People of all ranks and classes are equal in death, and nobody is exempt from dying.

292. **Desert and reward seldom keep company** .

People are often not rewarded for their good deeds or meritorious behavior; conversely, those who do receive rewards have often done nothing to deserve them.

293. **Desperate diseases must have desperate remedies.**

Drastic action is called for — and justified — when you find yourself in a particularly difficult situation.

294. Diamond cuts diamond.

The only match for a very sharp-witted or cunning person is somebody of equally sharp wit or great cunning.

295. Discretion is the better part of valor.

It is wise to be careful and not show unnecessary bravery. *Son: Can I go hand gliding with my friends? Father: No. Son: But they'll say I'm chicken if I don't go! Father: Discretion is the better part of valor, and I'd rather have them call you chicken than risk your life.*

296. DIY .

Do It Yourself. Describing actions taken that would usually be left to industrial bodies, synonymous to homemade, or tasks often of a manual labour nature, such as painting and decorating.

297. Do as I say, not as I do.

Do what somebody tells or advises you to do rather than what that person actually does himself or herself.

298. Do right and fear no man..

Criminals and other wrongdoers have a tendency to fear and suspect all those around them; sometimes used to imply that a distrustful person has something on his or her conscience.

299. Do unto others as you would have them do unto you.

Don't do mean things to people.

300. Dodgy .

Bad quality, untrustworthy or dysfunctional.

301. **Dog does not eat dog; there's honor among thieves..**

People who belong to the same group will not—or should not—harm one another.

302. **Do-Lally .**

Crazy but in a non offensive context.

303. **Don't bite off more than you can chew.**

Don't take more responsibility than you can handle.
I bit off more than I can chew when I said 'yes' to my boss for another project.

304. **Don't bite the hand that feeds you.**

Don't act badly toward the person who has helped you or from whom you derive some benefits, for you may lose those benefits in future.
Don't bite the hand that feeds you by talking ill of your mentor for such a small thing. If he distances himself from you or talk bad about you, it can hurt you bad.

305. **Don't cast pearls before swine.**

Don't offer something valuable to someone who doesn't value it.
To serve them French cuisine is like casting pearls before swine.

306. **Don't count your chickens before they hatch.**

Don't make plans based on future events that may not happen at all.
I've to prepare for my campaign. But you haven't been nominated yet. Don't count your chickens before they hatch.

307. **Don't cross a bridge until you come to it.**

Deal with a situation when it happens and not
unnecessarily worry about it in advance.
*I know you're worried about the mortgage payment in January,
but don't cross the bridge till you come to it.*

308. Don't cry before you're hurt .

There is no point in upsetting yourself about something
bad that may or may not happen.

309. Don't cut off your nose to spite your face.

Do not take action to spite others that will harm you more
than them.

310. Don't get mad, get even .

Take positive action to retaliate for a wrong that has been
done to you, rather than wasting your time and energy in
angry recriminations.

311. Don't hide your light under a bushel.

If you have special skills or talents, do not conceal them
through modesty and prevent others from appreciating or
benefiting from them.

312. Don't judge a book by its cover.

Just like you can't form an opinion of a book just by
looking at its cover, you can't form an opinion about
someone (or something) from their outward appearance.
*He seems a bit jerk to me, but, hey, you never know. He may be
good. You shouldn't judge a book by its cover.*

313. Don't kill the goose that lays the golden eggs.

If you kill a goose that lays golden eggs, you destroy
something that makes lot of money for you.
Tourists come to this city mainly to see this monument. By

opening it to commercial use, the city council may kill the goose that lays golden eggs.

314. Don't let the fox guard the hen house.

Do not put somebody in a position where he or she will be tempted to wrongdoing.

315. Don't make a mountain out of a molehill.

To exaggerate a small problem to make it seem like a major one.
One incorrect answer in the exam is not going to tank your grades. You're making a mountain out of a molehill.

316. Don't overload gratitude; if you do, she'll kick.

When people are grateful to you, do not take excessive advantage of the situation, because any sense of obligation has its limits.

317. Don't put all of your eggs in one basket.

Don't put all of your hopes and resources into one goal or dream
"I know you really want to be an actor, but don't you think you're being financially irresponsible? Don't put all of your eggs in one basket."

318. Don't put off until tomorrow what you can do today.

If you can do something today, do it. Don't wait until tomorrow; don't procrastinate.
"You have 6 hours of free time now. You should start on that final psychology assignment. Don't put off until tomorrow what you can do today."

319. Don't put the cart before the horse.

Do things in proper order. 'Horse before the cart' is the proper order, and not 'cart before the horse'.

Don't put the cart before the horse by finalizing the house you want to buy before you arrange the funds for down payment.

320. Don't put too many irons in the fire.

Don't try to do too many things at the same time; focus on one thing at a time
"No wonder you're exhausted. You're trying to work 4 jobs at the same time! You have too many irons in the fire right now."

321. Don't shout until you are out of the woods .

Avoid any show of triumph or relief until you are sure that a period of difficulty or danger is over.

322. Don't take down a fence unless you are sure why it was put up.

Most things were constructed or established for a purpose, and it is unwise to destroy or dismantle them unless you are certain that they are not longer required.

323. Don't talk the talk if you can't walk the walk.

Don't boast of something if you are unwilling or unable to back it up by your actions.

324. Don't teach your grandmother to suck eggs.

Do not presume to give advice or instruction to those who are older and more experienced than you.

325. Don't throw good money after bad.

If you have already spent money on a venture that seems likely to fail, do not waste any further money on it.

326. Don't throw out the baby with the bathwater.

Do not take the drastic step of abolishing or discarding something in its entirety when only part of it is unacceptable.

327. Don't throw the baby with the bathwater.

Don't discard something valuable while getting rid of something worthless.
We shouldn't scrap the entire project for a subpart not planned well. Let's not throw the baby with the bathwater.

328. Don't wash your dirty linen in public.

Do not discuss private disputes or family scandals in public.

329. Don't wish too hard; you might just get what you wished for.

Beware of wishing for something too much, because you might not like it when you get it.

330. Don't bite the hand that feeds you.

If someone's paying you or helping you out, you have to be careful not to make them angry or say bad things about them.

331. Don't count your chickens before they hatch.

Your plans might not work out, so don't start thinking about what you'll do after you succeed. Wait until you've already succeeded, and then you can think about what to do next.

332. Don't put all your eggs in one basket.

Have a backup plan. Don't risk all of your money or time in one plan.

333. Down to earth.

And adjective for practicality and lack of pretense.

334. Drag one's feet.

To do something slowly deliberately
The police is dragging its feet in investigating this case allegedly because influential people are involved in the crime.

335. Draw first blood.

If you draw first blood, you cause the first damage to an opponent in a conflict or contest.
Federer drew the first blood by breaking Anderson's service in the fourth game of the first set.

336. Dream of a funeral and you hear of a marriage.

According to popular superstition, if you dream about a funeral you will shortly receive news that somebody of your acquaintance is to be married

337. Dreams go by contraries..

According to popular superstition, if you dream about a funeral you will shortly receive news that somebody of your acquaintance is to be married

338. Drive a hard bargain.

If you drive a hard bargain, you argue hard to get a favorable deal.
The author tried to drive a hard bargain with the publisher on signing amount, but couldn't because he didn't have best sellers in his name.

339. Drive gently over the stones.

Take a cautious and delicate approach to any problems or difficulties you encounter in life.

340. Drive up the wall.

To irritate.

341. Drunkenness reveals what soberness conceals; there's truth in wine..

People have a tendency to talk too freely and become indiscreet when they are drunk.

342. Ducky .

Term of endearment, particularly for family, women and children.

343. Early bird catches the worm.

One who starts early on the work has higher chance of success.
Why have you come so early for the season-ending sale? So that I can choose from a wider selection and get a better piece. Early bird catches the worm, after all.

344. East is East and West is West and never the twain shall meet.

People who are very different in background or outlook are likely never to agree.

345. Easy come, easy go.

You say this when you get something easily and then lose it as easily.
I found fifty dollars while on my morning walk, but I frittered it away foolishly by the afternoon – easy come, easy go.

346. Easy Now .

A command to calm down or be more gentle.

347. Eat humble pie.

Be humiliated by admitting that you are wrong
The e-commerce company claimed that they'll surpass the market leader in two years, but they had to eat humble pie after the latest sales numbers.

348. Eat like a bird.

To eat little food
You claim to be eating like a bird for the past three months, but you've hardly lost any weight.

349. Eat like a horse.

If you eat like a horse, you eat a lot.
He is lean, but he eats like a horse.

350. Eat your words.

If you eat your words, you retract your statement or words.
Experts had to eat their words on the impending doom of abc.com when the fledgling ecommerce website turned in an unexpected profit.

351. Education doesn't come by bumping your head against the schoolhouse.

Education can only be acquired by studying, and by listening and talking to teachers.

352. Egg on your face.

If you've egg on your face, you look stupid and face embarrassment because of something you've done.
The case of the minister issuing statement in favor of a convicted person has left the government with egg on its face.

353. Empty vessels make the most noise..

Foolish people are the most talkative; often used as a put-down to somebody who chatters incessantly.

354. Enough is as good as a feast.

A moderate amount is sufficient; often said by somebody who does not want any more.

355. Equality begins in the grave..

People of all ranks and classes are equal in death, and nobody is exempt from dying.

356. Even a blind pig occasionally picks up an acorn.

An incompetent person or an unsystematic approach is bound to succeed every now and then by chance.

357. Even a worm will turn.

Even the most humble or submissive person will ultimately respond in anger to excessive harassment or exploitation.

358. Every bullet has its billet.

In a life threatening situation, destiny decides who will die and who will survive.

359. Every cloud has a silver lining.

Every bad or negative situation can result in some benefit to you. (The presence of silver lining means that the sun is behind the cloud and will eventually emerge.)
I know your business has suffered few setbacks this season. But remember, every cloud has a silver lining.

360. **Every dog has his day.**

Even the unluckiest or the most unfortunate will taste success at some point.
Are you surprised that John, the laggard, has got 92 percent marks in math? Well, every dog has his day.

361. **Every dog is allowed one bite.**

Somebody may be forgiven for a single misdemeanor, provided that it does not happen again

362. **Every employee tends to rise to his level of incompetence .**

People in a hierarchical organization are promoted until they reach a position that is just beyond their capabilities; this cynical observation implies that nobody is fit to do the work he or she is employed to do.

363. **Every horse thinks its own pack heaviest.**

Everybody thinks that he or she has harder work, greater misfortune, or more problems than others.

364. **Every man for himself and the devil take the hindmost .**

In highly competitive or dangerous situations, you must guard or pursue your own interests with ruthless disregard for those who are falling behind or struggling to cope.

365. **Every man has his price.**

Anyone can be swayed to do something. It's just that some may demand high price, some low.This proverb is also used in the sense of bribing people.
He has declined our offer to join the company. Sweeten the offer. Raise the compensation. Every man has his price.

366. **Every man must skin his own skunk.**

People should be self-reliant and not depend on others to do things — especially unpleasant tasks — for them.

367. **Every man thinks his own geese swans.**

Everybody tends to rate his or her own children, possessions, or achievements more highly than others would do.

368. **Every picture tells a story.**

Meaning is often conveyed by people's actions, movements, gestures, or facial expressions without the need for words.

369. **Every soldier has the baton of a field marshal in his knapsack .**

A common soldier, or any other worker, may aspire to senior rank.

370. **Every tub must stand on its own bottom.**

People should be self-sufficient and not dependent on others, financially or otherwise.

371. **Everybody has his fifteen minutes of fame.**

Most people will find themselves briefly in the public eye at least once in their lives.

372. **Everybody talks about the weather, but nobody does anything about it .**

People are always ready to complain about a problem but never willing to solve it.

373. **Everybody to whom much is given, of him will much be**

required.

> More is expected of those who have received more — that
> is, those who have had good fortune, are naturally gifted,
> or have been shown special favor.

374. Everybody's business is nobody's business.

> Matters that are of general concern,but are the
> responsibility of nobody in particular, tend to get
> neglected because everybody thinks that somebody else
> should deal with them.

375. Everybody's queer but you and me, and even you are a little queer.

> There are times when it seems that you are the only
> normal or sane person in the world.

376. Evil communications corrupt good manners.

> Good people can be led astray by listening to bad ideas,
> associating with bad people, or following a bad example.

377. Evil doers are evil dreaders.

> Criminals and other wrongdoers have a tendency to fear
> and suspect all those around them; sometimes used to
> imply that a distrustful person has something on his or her
> conscience.

378. Excuse me .

> Asking to be excused for a mistake, addressing a strangers
> attention, or asking someone to repeat themselves.

379. Experience is the best teacher..

> It is foolish to learn — or to expect other people to learn —
> solely by making mistakes; also used with the implication

that wise people learn from others' mistakes rather than their own.

380. Experience is the teacher of fools.

It is foolish to learn—or to expect other people to learn—solely by making mistakes; also used with the implication that wise people learn from others' mistakes rather than their own.

381. Extremes meet.

People and things that seem to be diametrically opposed are often found to have a point of contact.

382. Face the music.

If you face the music, you're at the receiving end of somebody's criticism or reprimand.
You'll face the music for deliberately reporting inflated sales numbers.

383. Fact is stranger than fiction.

Things that happen in real life are often far more unlikely than those dreamed up by writers.

384. Fag .

A cigarette.

385. Fall seven times.

Be resilient and try despite failures. That's how you succeed.
Abraham Lincoln lost so many elections, but he kept trying. Eventually he became the President of United States. It's rightly said: Fall seven times. Stand up eight.

386. Familiarity breeds contempt.

When you're around someone for too long, you get tired of them and annoyed by them.

387. Fancy .

A soft desire for something, including people, food and/or objects, activities, things.

388. Fancy passes beauty.

It is more important that a potential partner is likeable than good-looking.

389. Fear lends wings.

Fear inspires extra speed in those attempting to escape whatever threatens them.

390. Feed a cold and starve a fever .

You should eat well when you have a cold but fast when you have a fever

391. Feeling blue; have the blues.

A feeling of depression or sadness.

392. Fields have eyes and woods have ears.

There are very few places where you can do or say something without the risk of being seen or overheard.

393. Fine words butter no parsnips.

Promises or compliments are pleasant to hear but serve no practical purpose unless they are backed up by action.

394. First catch your hare.

Do not act in anticipation of something that is yet to be achieved.

395. First come, first served.

Those who arrive first will receive first.
The first 100 subscribers will receive an Amazon gift card. It's first come, first served.

396. First things first..

It is important to do things in the right or natural order; also used when people confuse cause and effect

397. First try and then trust.

Before relying upon something (or someone), it is best to test it first.

398. Fish or cut bait .

The time has come to choose between two courses of action — either get on with what you have to do, or go away and let somebody else do it

399. Fiver .

5 GBP (Great British Pound)

400. Flattery, like perfume, should be smelled but not swallowed.

There is no harm in taking pleasure from flattery, but do not make the mistake of believing it.

401. Flippin' .

A negative adjective, softer version of a swear word.

402. Fo' reals, brah! .

I'm telling you the truth, my friend. Slang for 'For Real!')

403. Food without hospitality is medicine.

It is hard to enjoy refreshments that are offered with ill grace, or without friendly companionship.

404. Fools and children should never see half done work.

You should not judge the quality of a piece of work until it is complete, because it often appears unpromising in its unfinished form; sometimes said in response to criticism, or as a reason for not letting such work be seen.

405. Fools build houses and wise men live in them.

The cost of building property is such that those who build houses cannot afford to live in them, and have to sell them to recoup their losses; also applied to other things that are expensive to produce

406. Fools rush in where angels fear to tread.

Fools or inexperienced persons get involved in situations or pursue goals without much thought. In contrast, wise are thoughtful about such situations or goals.
He sent an angry email without going into the background of the matter – fools rush in where angels fear to tread.

407. Foot in the door.

If you get your foot in the door, you succeed in achieving an initial step in an area that is difficult to succeed in.
It's your relationships that help in getting your foot in the door in the initial phase of your business. Otherwise, it can be a grind.

408. Footprints on the sands of time are not made by sitting down.

People who idle their lives away will not make a lasting impression on history or be remembered for their great achievements; used as a spur to action and industry.

409. For Real.

A proclamation of honesty.

410. For the birds.

Imagine how this phrase must sound to someone who doesn't understand that it refers to something that is substandard in some respect. Is it a bag of seeds or some kind of yard ornament reference? The Brits sometimes use the word 'bird,' to refer to women, in the same way Americans use 'chicks.' So, maybe it comes off like reference to girlishness. Who knows?

411. For want of a nail the shoe was lost, for want of a shoe the horse was lost, and for want of a horse the rider was lost.

Do not neglect minor details that seem insignificant in themselves.

412. Forbidden fruit is sweet .

Things that you must not have or do are always the most desirable.

413. Fortune favors the bold.

People who bravely go after what they want are more successful than people who try to live safely.

414. Fortune favors the brave.

If you carry out your plans boldly, the luck is more likely to favor you.
I know you're hesitant to accept the overseas position in your Company because the ground realities there are different from what you've faced so far, but remember fortune favors the brave.

415. Four eyes see more than two.

Two people keeping watch, supervising, or searching have a better chance of noticing or finding something.

416. Foxy Lady .

An attractive, seductive female.

417. Freaking Out .

Not quite panicking, but in an elevated state of confusion or discontent

418. From the horse's mouth.

If you hear from the horse's mouth, you hear from the original or trustworthy source.
We've lost the deal we bid for last month. It's true, because I've heard it from the horse's mouth – my manager.

419. From the sweetest wine, the tartest vinegar.

Great love may turn to the intense hatred; also used of other changes of feeling or nature from one extreme to the other.

420. Garbage in, garbage out.

A person or machine provided with inferior source material, faulty instructions, or erroneous information can produce only poor-quality work or rubbish.

421. Gather ye rosebuds while ye may.

Live life to the full while you are still young enough to enjoy it.

422. Gawp .

To stare with a gormless expression

423. Geezer .

Another male nickname typically used by males.

424. Genius is an infinite capacity for taking pains.

What appears to be a product of superior intellectual power is often simply the result of great assiduity and meticulous attention to detail.

425. Get out while the going (getting) is good.

To leave a place or situation before conditions worsen and it becomes difficult to leave.
With the stock market at an all-time high and further upside looking difficult, we decided sell our shares and get out while the going was good.

426. Get someone off the hook.

If you get someone off the hook, you help them get out of trouble.
The government has intervened by infusing billions of dollars to get the banks off the hook.

427. Give a beggar a horse and he'll ride it to death.

People who suddenly acquire wealth or power are likely to misuse it.

428. Give a dog a bad name and hang him..

Those who are planning some action that might attract criticism first seek to justify it in advance.

429. Give a loaf and beg a slice.

People who are too generous risk having to beg themselves.

430. Give a man an inch and he'll take a mile.

People are inclined to take excessive advantage of the tolerance or generosity of others; often used to warn against making even the smallest concession.

431. Give a man enough rope and he'll hang himself.

People who are given complete freedom of action will ultimately bring about their own downfall, for example by inadvertently revealing their guilt.

432. Give a ring.

To call someone on the telephone.

433. Give a thing, and take a thing, to wear the devil's gold ring.

It is wrong to take back a gift.

434. Give and take is fair play.

Exchanging like for like—whether it be a blow, an insult, a favor, or a pardon—is a fair and legitimate way to proceed.

435. Give me a child for the first seven years and he is mine for life..

Children and foolish people have a tendency to say what is true, because they have not learned that it may be advantageous or diplomatic to do otherwise.

436. Give someone a run for their money.

If you give someone a run for their money, you compete well with them.
Despite being an underdog, Division B team gave the best team of the tournament run for their money.

437. Give the devil his due.

People deserve recognition for their skills and contributions even if they are otherwise unworthy or unlikable.

438. Give them an inch and they'll take a mile.

If you give someone a small amount of power or freedom to do something, they may try to get a lot more.
He borrowed my car for a day, but hasn't returned even after four days. Well, give them an inch and they'll take a mile.

439. Gnashers .

Teeth

440. Go abroad and you'll hear news of home .

People often remain ignorant of matters concerning their family and friends, or events in their own neighborhood,until they go traveling, when they hear about them at second hand.

441. Go against the grain.

If an idea or action goes against the grain, you don't do it or accept it because it is against your beliefs or principle.
It goes against the grain these days to use polythene bags as carry bags.

442. Go farther and fare worse.

If you reject something acceptable in the hope of finding something better, you may end up having to settle for something worse.

443. Go in one ear and out the other.

If something you hear goes in one ear and out the other,
you quickly forget it.
Their advice to her went in one ear and out the other.

444. Go on record.

If you go on record about something, you say it publically
and officially. (You can't turn your back on such statement
later.)
*The actors have gone on record describing exploitation of
newcomers in the film industry.*

445. Go through the roof.

To increase beyond all expectations
Petrol and diesel prices have gone through the roof.

446. God helps those who help themselves.

Don't just wait for good things to happen to you. Work
hard to achieve your goals.
*You've to take the bull by horns and try getting a new job. God
helps those who help themselves.*

447. God made the country and man made the town .

The urban environment, constructed by human hands, is
inferior to the natural countryside, which is the work of
divine creation.

448. God never sends mouths but he sends meat.

God can be relied upon to provide for everybody.

449. God sends meat, but the devil sends cooks .

Good food can be ruined by a bad cook.

450. God tempers the wind to the shorn lamb.

Weak or vulnerable people have divine protection from the worst misfortunes; also used when such people are treated with compassion by their fellow human beings.

451. Going Dutch.

When each person, usually in a dating scenario, pays for his/her own meal.

452. Gold may be bought too dear.

Wealth is not worth having if there is too great a risk or sacrifice involved in acquiring it.

453. Good fences make good neighbors.

A good relationship between neighbors depends on each respecting the other's privacy and not entering his or her property uninvited; also used more broadly of international relations and the need to maintain trade barriers and border controls.

454. Good riddance to bad rubbish.

We are better off without worthless people or things; usually said on the departure of such a person or the loss of such a thing.

455. Good things come to those who wait.

Patience is often rewarded.
The best investors in the world have made their fortunes by investing for the long term. Good things come to those who wait.

456. Good wine needs no bush.

A good product does not need advertising.

457. Gormless .

Lacking in sense or initiative

458. Gossip is the lifeblood of society.

Social intercourse thrives on gossip — if people stopped talking about each other they might stop talking to each other.

459. Grace will last, beauty will blast.

A good character will outlive superficial physical attractiveness.

460. Great men have great faults.

Remarkable people tend to have serious character flaws.

461. Great trees keep down little ones.

The predominance of a particular person, company, nation, etc., results in lesser rivals being kept in the shade.

462. Grief divided is made lighter.

If you share your grief, it'll get easier to bear.
You shouldn't hold back the news of financial loss you've incurred in your business. Grief divided is made lighter.

463. Grub .

Food.

464. Gutted .

Extremely disappointed or upset.

465. Half a loaf is better than none.

Getting less than what one wants is better than not getting anything.
Did you get the compensation for damage to your vehicle? I was

hoping for $2,000, but the judge awarded only $800. Well, half a loaf is better than none.

466. Half the truth is often a whole lie.

Not telling the whole truth, or saying something that is only partly true, is tantamount to lying.

467. Hand in glove.

If you work hand in glove with someone, you work closely with them often to accomplish something dishonest.
Some of the bank employees have been allegedly working hand in glove with business owners to sanction loans without proper due diligence.

468. Handle with kid gloves.

If you handle someone with kid gloves, you treat them with extreme tact and care.
The client is hyper sensitive. We need to handle him with kid gloves, or we risk losing the deal.

469. Hang out.

To casually gather together or spend time with someone in a social manner.

470. Hanging and wiving go by destiny .

Some people are fated to marry each other, just as some are fated to be hanged.

471. Happy is the bride that the sun shines on.

According to popular superstition, a woman who has a sunny wedding day will have a happy marriage.

472. Happy is the country that has no history.

It is a happy or fortunate country that has no unpleasant events worth recording in its past.

473. Hard cases make bad law.

Cases that are complex or difficult to decide often cause the true meaning of the law to be distorted or obscured and sometimes lead to what is perceived as a miscarriage of justice.

474. Hard words break no bones.

Adverse criticism or verbal abuse may be unpleasant, but it does no physical harm.

475. Haste makes waste..

When you try to do things too quickly you work less efficiently and ultimately take longer.

476. Hasty climbers have sudden falls..

Foolish people act hastily and thus waste their efforts.

477. Have a thick skin.

To be less affected by criticisms and rebuffs
You need to have a thick skin to survive in politics.

478. Have one's cake and eat it too.

To have two good things at the same time that are incompatible and therefore not feasible
You don't want to pay more taxes and still have better services. You can't have your cake and eat it too.

479. Have one's hands full.

To be extremely busy
Working on two projects, I've my hands full.

73

480. Have the last laugh.

If you've the last laugh in an argument or disagreement, you ultimately succeed from a seemingly losing position.
He was dropped from the team, but he had the last laugh when he was recruited by a rival club at a higher fee.

481. Have your heart in your mouth.

If you've your heart in mouth, you're feeling extremely nervous.
My heart was in my mouth when he slipped and fell down on the floor.

482. Have your work cut out.

If you've your work cut out to do something, you've a difficult task at hand.
The government has its work cut out in controlling air pollution this winter.

483. Hawks will not pick out hawks' eyes.

People who belong to the same group will not — or should not — harm one another.

484. He comes too early who brings bad news.

People are never in a hurry to hear bad news.

485. He gives twice who gives quickly.

A prompt response to a request for something,such as money or help, is of greater value than a more generous offering given late.

486. He looks rode hard and put up wet .

He looks terrible.This comes from a reference to a horse that has been worked or ridden hard and then put back in the stall without being curried or wiped down.)

487. He that complies against his will is of his own opinion still.

By forcing somebody to do something, or to admit that something is true, you have not actually succeeded in changing that person's mind.

488. He that has a full purse never wanted a friend.

Wealthy people never lack friends — or those who claim to be their friends until their money runs out.

489. He that is too secure is not safe.

Beware of complacency — you must remain alert and watchful if you want to avoid danger

490. He that lives in hope dances to an ill tune.

It is unwise to let your future happiness or well-being depend on expectations that may not be realized.

491. He that lives on hope will die fasting.

do not pin all your hopes on something you may not attain, because you could end up with nothing.

492. He that touches pitch shall be defiled.

If you get involved with wicked people or illegal activities, you cannot avoid becoming corrupted yourself.

493. He that will not when he may, when he will he may have nay.

Take advantage of an opportunity when it presents itself, even if you do not want or need it at the time, because it may no longer be available when you do.

494. He that will thrive must first ask his wife.

A married man's financial situation, his success or failure in business, and the like often depend on the behavior and disposition of his wife.

495. He that would go to sea for pleasure would go to hell for a pastime.

A sailor's life can be so unpleasant and dangerous, it seems that those who choose spend their leisure hours at sea must be either masochistic or insane.

496. He that would hang his dog gives out first that he is mad.

Those who are planning some action that might attract criticism first seek to justify it in advance.

497. He that would have eggs must endure the cackling of hens.

You must be prepared to put up with something unpleasant or annoying in order to get what you want; also used of an undesirable aspect or drawback that accompanies something.

498. He who excuses himself accuses himself..

People who seek to blame the times or conditions they live in are really trying to avoid taking the blame themselves

499. He who fights and runs away may live to fight another day.

It is wiser to withdraw from a situation that you cannot win than to go on fighting and lose — by a strategic retreat you can return to the battle or argument with renewed energy at a later date.

500. He who laughs last, laughs longest.

Minor successes or failures along the way are of no significance—the person who is ultimately triumphant is the only real winner; often used when somebody turns the tables with a final act of retaliation.

501. He who pays the piper calls the tune.

The person who pays for a service or finances a project has the right to say how it should be done.

502. He who rides a tiger is afraid to dismount.

When you are in a dangerous situation, or have embarked on a dangerous course of action, it is often safer to continue than to try to stop or withdraw.

503. He who sups with the devil should have a long spoon.

Those who have dealings with wicked, dangerous, or dishonest people should remain on their guard and try not to become too intimately involved.

504. He who wills the end, wills the means.

Those who are determined to achieve something are equally determined to find a way of achieving it.

505. He who would write and can't write can surely review.

People who become critics are those who lack the talent to be novelists, dramatists, or other kinds of artists in their own right; used in response to a bad review.

506. Head and shoulders above.

Greatly superior to
In his prime, Usain Bolt was head and shoulders above his competitors.

507. Head in the clouds.

If your head is in the clouds, you're not in touch with the ground realities.
Many academics have their heads in the clouds.

508. Head over heels.

If you're head over heels, you're completely in love.
Max fell head over heels in love with her colleague and wants to marry her.

509. Heads I win, tails you lose.

In some situations it is impossible for one person not to be a winner — or impossible for another person not to be a loser — whatever the outcome.

510. Hear all, see all, say nothing.

It is sometimes prudent to listen and watch carefully, but say nothing.

511. Heart misses (skips) a beat.

If your heart misses a beat, you feel excited or nervous.
My heart skipped few beats while scrolling down the exam result on the notice board.

512. Hell hath no fury like a woman scorned.

A woman who is rejected by the man she loves has an immense capacity for ferocious or malicious revenge.

513. Hell .

Extreme, such as 'hell of a storm', or an addition to an exclamation such as 'bloody hell'

514. Help you to salt, help you to sorrow .

According to popular superstition, it is unlucky to add salt to another person's food at table.

515. Her Majesty's Pleasure .

Being locked up in prison for life.

516. History is a fable agreed upon.

History represents the traditionally accepted interpretation of what actually happened in the past.

517. Hit the book.

To study
I need to hit the book today or else I'll fall behind in my exam prep.

518. Hit the bottle.

To drink alcohol to excess
He doesn't hit the bottle often, but when he does, he can be nasty.

519. Hit the jackpot.

If you hit the jackpot, you achieve big success, usually through luck.
We've hit the jackpot with our new product – sales have doubled.

520. Hit the nail on the head.

If you hit the nail on the head, you're exactly right about something.
I think the CEO hit the nail on the head when he said that the organization was losing market share because of complacency and security.

521. Hit the sack.

To go to bed
I hit the sack around 11 PM.

522. Hitch your wagon to a star.

You must be ambitious, and aim to achieve the highest possible goal; also used as advice to cultivate the acquaintance of powerful, successful, or influential people who can help to advance your interests.

523. Hold your horses.

Be patient
Hold your horses! I'm not yet done with my explanation.

524. Hold your tongue.

To hold your tongue means to not speak
"Hold your tongue, son. Be patient," the old man tried to restrain the agitated man.

525. Home is home, be it ever so homely.

However simple or lowly a person's abode may be, it is still his or her home and therefore the best place to be.

526. Homer sometimes nods.

Even the greatest minds have lapses of attention, leading to mistakes; often used as an excuse for error

527. Honest men marry quickly, wise men not at all.

Honest men marry without hesitation, seeing no threat in a wife, but wise men know better.

528. Honesty is the best policy.

It's always better to be truthful and honest, even if the opposite may get you the benefits.
I think you should just explain what happened, rather than trying to cover your tracks. Honesty is the best policy, after all.

529. Honors change manners .

People who improve their status in society all too often become arrogant.

530. Hope for the best, prepare for the worst.

Be optimistic, but be prepared for a scenario where things can go wrong.
We're hoping to raise capital from investors, but it may not come so soon. Therefore, it's imperative to look for alternatives as well. Let's hope for the best, but prepare for the worst.

531. Hope is a good breakfast but a bad supper.

There is no harm in being optimistic at the beginning of something, but beware of being left with nothing but unrealized expectations at the end.

532. Hope springs eternal in the human breast.

It is human nature to remain optimistic — even after a setback, or despite evidence to the contrary.

533. Horses for courses.

Different people have different strengths and talents, and each person should be assigned to the task or job that is best suited to that particular individual.

534. Humble hearts have humble desires.

People with timid characters tend to have modest ambitions.

535. Hunger drives the wolf out of the wood .

People in dire need are forced to do things that would be unwise or undesirable in other circumstances.

536. Hunger is the best sauce.

Hunger makes all food taste good, regardless of its quality or the way it is served.

537. Hurry no man's cattle.

Do not try to make others hurry or rush because you are impatient.

538. Hyped (adj.

A very excited state.

539. I was so scared, I about wet my pants! .

Although this has actually been known to happen literally, people often say this when it didn't really happen to stress how frightened they were.The 'about' is short for 'just about' or 'almost')

540. I'll Give You What For! .

An old expression meaning I'll hurt you, born out of a response to disobedience. I.e the disobedient one in response to an instruction such as 'go do this' replies 'what for?' so the instructor

541. If a pig had wings, it might fly.

Do not make plans based on things that cannot possibly happen.

542. If and an spoils many a good charter.

Excellent plans may be doomed to failure because of the conditions that come with them.

543. If ifs and ans were pots and pans, there'd be no work for

tinkers.

> Do not make plans based on things that cannot possibly happen.

544. If it ain't broke, don't fix it.

> If something is working fine, don't change it unnecessarily. *Why do you want to change this component in the machine when everything is working fine? OK. I agree. If it ain't broke, don't fix it.*

545. If it looks like a duck, walks like a duck, and quacks like a duck, it's a duck .

> It is usually safe to identify somebody as a particular type of person when his or her appearance, behavior, and words all point to the same conclusion.

546. If one sheep leaps over the ditch, all the rest will follow .

> Where one person sets an example by doing something risky or dangerous others are likely to follow.

547. If the mountain won't come to Muhammad, Muhammad must go to the mountain.

> If things don't turn the way you want them to, then adjust your way to suit those things.
> *I need that book for completing my assignment. If you aren't coming to the college tomorrow, I'll come to your place to take it – if the mountain won't come to Muhammad, Muhammad must go to the mountain.*

548. If the shoe fits, wear it.

> If it seems that a critical remark applies to you, then you must accept it; often said when somebody's response to a general remark suggests that it is appropriate to that particular person.

549. If the sky falls, we shall catch larks.

Do not make plans based on things that cannot possibly happen.

550. If two ride on a horse, one must ride behind.

When two people undertake a joint activity or enterprise, one of them invariably takes the lead and the other has to be content with a more subordinate role; also used of a fight argument, where only one can win and the other must lose or surrender.

551. If wishes were horses, beggars would ride..

Do not make plans based on things that cannot possibly happen.

552. If you can't beat 'em, join 'em.

If you can't change someone's behavior or opinion, sometimes it's better or easier to do what they want to do *"I told Mark that we needed to study, but he kept playing video games. Eventually I gave up and just played video games too. If you can't beat 'em, join 'em."*

553. If you can't bite, never show your teeth.

Do not make empty threats; also used to warn against making a show of aggression when you unable to defend yourself.

554. If you can't run with the big dogs, stay under the porch.

If you lack the strength, courage, skill, or experience to compete with the major players — in politics, business, or any other field — then it is better not to try at all.

555. If you can't beat 'em, join 'em.

When you try to change someone's behavior and it doesn't work, you might have to change instead. For example, if you're trying to get your classmates to focus on studying but they want to party, maybe you should just party with them.

556. **If you don't like it, you can lump it .**

Whether or not you like what is offered or approve of what is proposed, you will have to put up with it.

557. **If you don't sit still, I'm gonna hog-tie you! .**

A hog being readied for the slaughter sometimes has all four legs tied tightly together so it won't kick.)

558. **If you pay peanuts, you get monkeys.**

Competent and highly qualified people will not work for derisory fees or wages.

559. **If you play with fire, you'll get burned.**

If you do something dangerous or adventurous, you may get harmed.
Enacting the stunts of movie superheroes in real life is playing with fire. You may get burned.

560. **If you play with fire, you'll get burned.**

If you get involved in something dangerous or beyond your abilities, you will probably experience negative consequences
"Don't make him angry. If you play with fire, you'll get burned."

561. **If you want peace, prepare for war .**

A nation that is seen to be ready and able to defend itself — for example, with strong armed forces and powerful weapons — is less likely to be attacked.

562. If you want something done right, you have to do it yourself.

> Don't depend on someone else to do a good job; do it yourself
> *"I asked my roommate to wash the dishes, but they ended up super filthy! I guess it's true what they sa if you want something done right, you have to do it yourself."*

563. If you've got it, flaunt it.

> Those who have wealth, beauty, or talent should not be ashamed to show it off; used as an excuse for ostentation.

564. Ignorance is a voluntary misfortune.

> Everybody has the opportunity to acquire knowledge, so you have only yourself to blame if you remain ignorant.

565. Ignorance is bliss.

> If you don't know about something, you don't need to bother about it. In other words, if you're unaware of something, it won't cause you stress.This proverb, however, is often used in negative way – ignorance is not bliss.
> *I didn't know that the neighbor next door was involved in criminal activities. Sometimes, ignorance is bliss.*

566. Ill weeds grow apace.

> Worthless people or evil things have a tendency to flourish where better ones fail.

567. I'm fixin' to .

> I am about to; I am getting ready to.

568. In cold blood.

If you do something violent and cruel in cold blood, you do it deliberately and in an unemotional way.
He was murdered in cold blood.

569. In for a penny, in for a pound.

Once you have committed yourself to something, you might as well do it wholeheartedly and see it through to the end.

570. In full swing.

If something happens in full swing, it happens at the highest speed or level of activity.
Our development team is working in full swing to meet the deadline.

571. In politics a man must learn to rise above principle.

A successful politician cannot afford to have too many scruples; a cynical observation.

572. In the red (In the black).

Operating at a loss or under debt (Operating at a profit or have surplus)
Many airlines across the world are in the red because of increase in oil prices.

573. In the same boat.

If two or more persons are in the same boat, they're in the same difficult situation.
Both of us are in the same boat – without jobs.

574. In the same breath.

When you say two things in the same breath, you say two very different or contradictory things.
How can the manager praise my colleague and talk of his average performance in the same breath?

575. In war there is no substitute for victory.

A war is only truly won by total defeat of the enemy, not by diplomatic negotiations or compromise.

576. Is it in your road? .

Is something bothering you? Is something keeping you from going forward with your life? Also heard as 'Is it in your way?'

577. It ain't over till the fat lady sings.

This is an allusion to opera where the final big number is sung by the soprana.

578. It never rains but it pours.

One setback, misfortune, or other undesirable occurrence is inevitably followed by many more; also occasionally used of pleasant things, such as a run of good luck.

579. It takes a village to raise a child.

The whole community plays a part in the upbringing of the children that live there.

580. It takes one to know one.

Only those with similar flaws are capable of spotting them in others.

581. It takes two to make a quarrel.

An argument of quarrel is not one person's fault.
Why are you always so quarrelsome? I'm not the only person involved. It takes two to make a quarrel.

582. It takes two to tango.

Where two parties are involved in a situation, fault usually lies with both if things go wrong. Rarely can one party be blamed entirely.
This deal won't go through unless you too are willing to compromise. It takes two to tango, after all.

583. **It's a foolish sheep that makes the wolf his confessor .**

Do not confide in somebody unless you are certain that he or she can be trusted.

584. **It's a long road that has no turning; the longest day must have an end..**

No matter how tiring or stressful a day you are having,you can console yourself with the fact that it will eventually be over; also used more generally to recommend perseverance or endurance in a trying situation.

585. **It's a poor dog that's not worth whistling for.**

Everybody has some value, or some redeeming feature.

586. **It's all in a day's work.**

Unpleasant things have to be accepted as part of the daily routine; also used to play down a major achievement or a heroic act by implying that it is just part of your job.

587. **It's an ill bird that fouls its own nest.**

You should not say or do anything that will bring discredit or harm to your own family or country.

588. **It's better to be happy than wise.**

Happiness is more important than wisdom, knowledge, or learning.

589. It's better to be safe than sorry.

It's better to be cautious than regret later.
One shouldn't complain about the inconvenience of security check each time you enter the building. It's better to be safe than sorry.

590. It's better to lose the battle and win the war.

It is sometimes prudent or expedient to concede a minor point in an argument or dispute in order to gain the overall victory.

591. It's dogged as does it.

Anything can be done with determination and perseverance.

592. It's easier to tear down than to build up..

Something that has taken time, skill, and effort to put together can be quickly ruined or destroyed by a foolish person.

593. It's easy to be wise after the event.

It is easy to understand what you could have done to prevent something bad from happening after it has happened.
I would have never bought an apartment if I had known that the land on which it has been built is disputed. Well, it's easy to be wise after the event.

594. It's easy to find a stick to beat a dog.

It is easy to find some reason or excuse to justify a critical attack or a harsh punishment.

595. It's good to make a bridge of gold to a flying enemy.

Retreating enemies will kill or destroy anybody or anything that stands in their way, so it is advisable to give them free passage.

596. It's idle to swallow the cow and choke on the tail.

Once you have completed the major part of an enterprise or undertaking, it is foolish not to see it through to the end.

597. It's ill jesting with edged tools.

Do not trifle with dangerous things or people.

598. It's ill sitting at Rome and striving with the Pope.

It is foolish or pointless to quarrel or fight with somebody who has supreme power in the place where you are.

599. It's ill speaking between a full man and a fasting.

Hungry people are not on the best of terms with those who have eaten their fill.

600. It's ill waiting for dead men's shoes.

It is not good to be impatiently awaiting somebody's death or retirement to get what you want, such as an inheritance or promotion.

601. It's never too late to mend.

It's never too late to change your wrong ways or habits. *I still miss my best friend, but it's been a year since our fight and we haven't spoken to each other since. Well, it's never too late to mend; why don't you call him up and apologize?*

602. It's no use crying over spilt milk.

There is no point in staying upset over a mistake because you can't undo what has happened.

He is feeling terrible for accidently elbowing the flower pot from the window. It's broken now. It's no use crying over spilt milk.

603. It's not the end of the world.

Things are not as disastrous as they seem; said in recurrence, such as after a minor mishap.

604. It's the last straw that breaks the camel's back.

When somebody is close to his or her limit of patience or endurance, it takes only one little extra thing to make the whole load too much to bear.

605. It's the tip of the iceberg.

If you say something is tip of the iceberg, you mean that thing is just a small part of the entire thing.
The flooding is bad, but we're dealing with just the tip of the iceberg – water-borne diseases are waiting to break out.

606. Jack of all trades, master of none.

A handyman that can do many things, but none of them well.
Joe is a Jack of all trades, but a master of none.

607. Jack up.

An abrupt increase, typically in the price of something.

608. Jack's as good as his master.

No person is born superior or inferior to another, so all should have equal rights.

609. Jam tomorrow and jam yesterday, but never jam today.

Good times always seem to belong to the past or to the future, but never to the present.

610. Jesters do oft prove prophets.

A prediction made in jest often comes true.

611. John Hancock.

The name John Hancock became synonymous with a person's signature because his was one of the more flamboyant signatures on The Declaration of Independence.

612. Jolly Good .

Very good

613. Jonesing.

To want, crave, or desire something intensely, and its noun form, 'joneser,' (a person who wants or craves something intensely), isn't always apparent even to Americans.The Oxford Dictionary associates this word's slang usage with Jones Alley in Manhattan, a haven for drug addicts in the 1960s.The unsavory drug culture connotations continue today. However the definition of 'joneser,' has been broadened among some circles to include describing a person whose character is found wanting, i.e. Lacking, as opposed to someone who simply wants something desperately.

614. Jove but laughs at lovers' perjury.

The breaking of oaths and promises made by lovers is so commonplace that it is not regarded as a serious matter

615. Jump the gun.

To do something too soon without proper thought
I jumped the gun by sending the proposal to the client without first showing it to my manager.

616. Justice is blind.

Justice must be dispensed with objectivity and without regard to irrelevant details or circumstances.

617. Keep a thing seven years and you'll find a use for it.

An object that seems useless now may be just what you need at some future time, so do not discard it.

618. Keep an ear to the ground.

Be well informed of current trends, opinions, and happenings
One of the main reasons for his success in business is that he keeps an ear to the ground to know what the customers want and why they're dissatisfied with competing products.

619. Keep one's words.

To do as promised
He always keeps his words. If he has promised to put in a word for you, he will.

620. Keep someone at arm's length.

If you keep someone at arm's length, you avoid becoming friendly with them.
I've more productive time in the day because I've developed this good habit of keeping video games at arm's length.

621. Keep your eyes wide open before marriage, half shut afterward .

You should choose your husband or wife with care, but be prepared to overlook his or her faults after the wedding day.

622. Keep your friends close and your enemies closer.

If you have an enemy, pretend to be friends with them instead of openly fighting with them.That way you can watch them carefully and figure out what they're planning.

623. Keep your mouth shut and your eyes open.

Speak only when necessary and remain alert and observant at all times.
We're in a hostile territory. So, to avoid problems, keep your mouth shut and your eyes open.

624. Keep Calm and Carry On .

Not really slang, but the text of a very common poster during WWII, which is now wide spread and vastly readapted to different contexts.

625. Kill the goose that lays the golden eggs.

To destroy something that gives you lot of money to get immediate returns
Thomas killed the goose that laid the golden eggs when he sold off his business before setting up another.

626. Kill two birds with one stone.

To achieve two goals with a single effort
I can kill two birds with a stone by picking up the laundry while going to the college.

627. Killing no murder..

Drastic action is called for — and justified — when you find yourself in a particularly difficult situation.

628. Kings have long arms.

Few people, places, or things are beyond the reach of those in authority, and it is not easy for an offender to escape capture or punishment.

629. Kissing goes by favor.

People often bestow honors and privileges on those they like, rather than on those who are most worthy of them.

630. Knackered .

Physically or mentally exhausted, tired.

631. Knock.

To speak negatively, to disparage, to badmouth.

632. Knockers .

The female bosoms.

633. Know which way the wind is blowing.

If you know which way the wind is blowing, you anticipate how certain situation is likely to develop. *Politicians are good at knowing which way the wind is blowing, and they form alliances with other political parties accordingly.*

634. Knowledge and timber shouldn't be much used until they are seasoned.

Knowledge is not useful until it is tempered by experience.

635. Knowledge is power.

The more you know, the more powerful you can be in different areas of your life
"When we were kids, our parents taught us how to swim.That knowledge helped me to save my cousin's life when he was 5 years old. Knowledge is power."

636. Late children, early orphans.

Children to older parents run a greater risk of being orphaned before they reach adulthood

637. Laugh all the way to the bank.

To earn lot of money by doing something which others thought to be a foolish pursuit
Investors dismissed his idea as immature, but he is now laughing all the way to the bank.

638. Laughter is the best medicine.

Thinking positively and laughing will help you to feel better.
I think the best thing for you right now would be to spend some time with people you can joke around with. Laughter is the best medicine, after all.

639. Laughter is the best medicine..

When you're in a difficult situation, laughing can make it easier to get through that situation
"I'm sorry to hear about your dog. Want to watch a funny movie? Sometimes, laughter is the best medicine."

640. Learn from the mistakes of others..

It is foolish to learn — or to expect other people to learn — solely by making mistakes; also used with the implication that wise people learn from others' mistakes rather than their own.

641. Learn to walk before you run.

Learn basic skills first before venturing into complex things.
I want to submit my first article to Fortune magazine for publication. I think I you should aim for smaller publications to start with. You should learn to walk before you run.

642. Least said, soonest mended .

The less you say, the less likely you are to cause trouble;
often used to discourage somebody from complaining,
apologizing, arguing, or making excuses.

643. Leave no stone unturned.

To do everything you can to achieve your goal
I left no stone unturned to raise money for my company.

644. Leave well enough alone.

Be well informed of current trends, opinions, and
happenings

645. Left out in the cold.

If you're left out in the cold, you're ignored.
*I was left out in the cold in the annual promotions in the
company.*

646. Lend your money and lose your friend.

You risk losing your friends by lending them money,
either because they fail to repay the loan or because they
resent being asked to repay it.

647. Length begets loathing.

Nobody likes a long-winded speaker or writer.

648. Less is more.

A work of art, piece of writing, or other creative endeavor
can be made more elegant or effective by reducing
ornamentation and avoiding excess.

649. Let not the sun go down on your wrath.

Deal with a situation when it happens and not
unnecessarily worry about it in advance.
Bible Reference: Ephesians 4:26

650. Let off steam.

To do or say something that helps you release pent-up
emotions such as anger or frustration
*When I get stressed at work, I go on a weekend trek to let off
steam.*

651. Let one's hair down.

To be relaxed and behave informally
*Over tea on Sunday, he finally let his hair down and talked
about his hobbies and family.*

652. Let sleeping dogs lie.

Don't talk about a bad situation people have forgotten and
that could unnecessarily create problem in the present.
*Should I ask the professor if he is upset about my late submission
of the assignment? If he hasn't said anything, then don't bring
forth the topic – let sleeping dogs lie.*

653. Let the cobbler stick to his last.

People should not offer advice, make criticisms, or
otherwise interfere in matters outside their own area of
knowledge or expertise.

654. Let the dead bury the dead.

Do not concern yourself with things that are past and
gone.
Bible Reference: Matthew 8:22

655. Let them laugh that win .

Do not rejoice until you are certain of victory or success.

656. Let your head save your heels.

You can avoid wasted journeys on foot by careful planning or forethought, such as by combining errands.

657. Liberty is not license..

Freedom does not mean that a person can whatever he or she wants.

658. Life is hard by the yard, but by the inch life's a cinch.

Life is less overwhelming if you take it one step at a time.

659. Light at the end of tunnel.

If you see light at the end of tunnel, you see signs of improvement in a situation that has been bad for a long time.
The business has started to gain momentum after months of struggle. We finally see light at the end of tunnel.

660. Light gains make heavy purses.

It is possible to become rich by making small profits.

661. Lighten up.

To relax and take things too seriously. Typically stated as an appeal to someone who is acting uptight.

662. Lightning never strikes twice in the same place.

Misfortune does not occur twice in the same way to the same person.
Example: I don't want to take this route, because I was robbed the last time I traveled on this route. Don't worry, lightning never strikes twice in the same place.

663. Like a cat on hot tin roof.

In an uneasy or nervous state
Waiting for the result of my medical tests, I was like a cat on hot tin roof.

664. Like a fish out of water.

If you're like a fish out of water in certain situation, you feel awkward because you haven't experienced that situation before.
I was like fish out of water when I moved to the capital from my hometown.

665. Like father, like son.

Said when a son is similar to his father; also, "Like mother, like daughter"
"Ryan started playing hockey at a very young age. He's just like his dad. Like father, like son."

666. Like father, like son; like mother, like daughter..

Children resemble their parents in character and nature.

667. Like people, like priest.

The quality of a spiritual leader can be judged by the behavior of his or her followers.

668. Listeners never hear any good of themselves.

People who eavesdrop on the conversations of others risk hearing unfavorable comments about themselves; used as a warning or reprimand.

669. Little birds that can sing and won't sing must be made to sing.

Those who refuse to tell what they know must be forced to do so; also interpreted more literally.

670. Little fish are sweet.

The smallest things are sometimes the most desirable or acceptable; used specifically of something received, bought, or otherwise acquired.

671. Little pitchers have big ears.

Children miss little of what is said in their hearing; often used as a warning.

672. Little strokes fell great oaks.

Great things can be achieved in small stages, or with persistent effort.

673. Little thieves are hanged, but great ones escape.

It is often the case that petty criminals are brought to justice, while those involved in more serious crimes succeed in evading capture and punishment.

674. Little things please little minds.

Foolish people are easily pleased; said contemptuously to or of somebody who is amused by something childish or trivial.

675. Live on borrowed time.

If you live on borrowed time, you continue to exist longer than expected.
This 15-year-old car is living on borrowed time.

676. Loaded .

Wealthy, rich or having a lot of money.

677. Long foretold, long last; short notice, soon past .

A change in the weather that is predicted well in advance lasts longer than one that arrives with little warning.

678. Look before you leap.

Consider all consequences before taking an action, especially when you can't retract.
I'm planning to pursue an MBA. It's an expensive degree and, moreover, you'll be out of work for two years. I would say look before you leap.

679. Look for needle in a haystack.

Looking for something small in a pile of other things or a vast area
The gem in my ring fell somewhere on my way to home. Finding it is like looking for a needle in a haystack.

680. Lookers-on see most of the game.

An objective observer with an overall view of a situation is often more knowledgeable, or better placed to make a judgment, than somebody who is actively involved, and whose attention is therefore focused on individual details.

681. Loony/Loopy .

A mad or crazy person.

682. Lose an hour in the morning, chase it all day.

Time lost in the morning is impossible to make up later in the day.

683. Lose your temper.

If you lose temper, you become very angry.
When he started giving excuse for not completing the assignment in time, the teacher lost her temper.

684. **Lost the Plot .**

Gone crazy, not following the situation.

685. **Love is free.**

People tend to fall in love regardless of the suitability of the match or other obstacles.

686. **Love laughs at locksmiths.**

Nothing and nobody can keep lovers apart.

687. **Love me little, love me long.**

Warm affection lasts longer than burning passion.

688. **Love me, love my dog.**

If you love somebody, you must be prepared to accept or tolerate everything and everybody connected with that person — his or her failings, idiosyncrasies, friends, relatives, and so on.

689. **Love thy neighbour as thyself.**

Treat others with the same respect you expect to receive.
Bible Reference: Matthew 22:39

690. **Love your enemy, but don't put a gun in his hand.**

Treat your enemies with respect and humanity, but also with caution — do not give them the opportunity to repay your kindness with an act of aggression.

691. **Lovely-Jubbly .**

Equal to 'lovely', a positive exclamation.

692. Make a mountain of a molehill.

If you make a mountain of a molehill, you make something unimportant to seem important.
One bad interview doesn't mean you're struggling to get the job. Don't make a mountain of a molehill.

693. Make a virtue of necessity.

The best way to handle an undesirable situation is to turn it to your advantage.

694. Make an offer one can't refuse.

Make such an attractive proposition that it would be foolhardy for anyone to refuse it.
The competitor offered $6 billion for our company. It was an offer we couldn't refuse.

695. Make haste slowly.

Do not rush — you will achieve your end more quickly if you proceed with care.

696. Make hay while the sun shines.

Make the most of favorable conditions till they last.
I got plenty of referral traffic to my website from Facebook in its initial years. I made hay while the sun shone. Later on they changed their algorithm, after which the traffic dried.

697. Make no bones about something.

If you make no bones about something, you say clearly what you feel or think about it.
Jack made no bones about getting a hike in his salary.

698. Make one's blood boil.

To make someone extremely angry
An excessive penalty for just one-day delay in payment of the bill made my blood boil.

699. Malarkey .

Stuff, or the subject of conversation. 'What's all that malarkey they were discussing?'

700. Man is the measure of all things.

Human beings are capable of rising to any challenge

701. Man's extremity is god's opportunity.

People are prone to calling on God in times of trouble, only to forget all about their newly found religious faith as soon as the crisis is past.

702. Many a little makes a mickle.

Small amounts accumulate to form a large quantity; often used of small sums of money saved over a long period.

703. Many a mickle makes a muckle.

Small amounts accumulate to form a large quantity; often used of small sums of money saved over a long period.

704. Many a true word is spoken in jest.

Something said jokingly often proves to be true.

705. Many are called but few are chosen.

Not everybody who wants to do something is selected or permitted to do it; used in any elitist situation.
Bible Reference: Matthew 22:14

706. Many go out for wool and come home shorn.

Many people who set out to make their fortune, or to achieve some other aim, end up in a worse state than before.

707. Many kiss the hand they wish to see cut off. Being deceived by such a show..

A person's true feelings or intentions may be concealed by the mask of politeness or hypocrisy; used to warn against

708. March winds and April showers always bring May flowers.

Something unpleasant often leads to something more desirable.

709. Marriage is a lottery. .

Whether a marriage succeeds or fails is all a matter of luck; also applied to the choice of a marriage partner.

710. Marriages are made in heaven..

Some people are fated to marry each other, just as some are fated to be hanged.
Theirs was a marriage made in Heaven.

711. Marry in haste, repent at leisure..

Those who rush into marriage, and subsequently discover that they have made a mistake,may have to live with the unpleasant consequences for a long time.

712. May chickens come cheeping.

Children born in the month of May are weak and delicate.

713. Meat and mass never hindered man..

You can always find time to eat and to go to church; said to somebody who claims to be too busy, or in too much of a hurry, for one or both of these.

714. **Meh** .

21st century exclamation of little consideration, equal to 'who cares?'

715. **Men are from Mars, women are from Venus.**

Men and women have essentially dissimilar nature

716. **Mint** .

An item in perfect condition.

717. **Minted** .

Very wealthy.

718. **Misery loves company.** .

When you are unhappy, it is good to be with others who have suffered in a similar way, or simply with people who will listen to your woes and offer sympathy; also used to imply that everybody around them to be in the same situation.

719. **Misery makes strange bedfellows; poverty makes strange bedfellows..**

In times of hardship or misfortune people often befriend or form alliances with those whose company they would normally avoid

720. **Miss the boat/ bus.**

To miss an opportunity
He waited far too long to get a good deal. Most good ones are gone now. He missed the boat.

721. **Monday morning quarterback.**

Because quarterback is an on-field leadership position played in American football, which the British have no interest in, and because Monday morning references the fact that most NFL games take place on Sundays, this is a doubly obscure metaphor. While American's understand that the phrase references the practice of criticizing something after-fact-with the advantage of hindsight, an English person would find this phrase totally meaningless.

722. Money burns a hole in the pocket. .

People are often too eager to spend their money.

723. Money doesn't grow on trees.

Spend money carefully because it's limited. You can't grow it on trees and replenish.
I'm surprised that you spent your entire month's salary on a frivolous gadget. Well, money doesn't grow on trees.

724. Money has no smell. Anywhere else.

Money that comes from unsavory or questionable sources is no different from — and no less acceptable than — money that comes from

725. Money talks.

Money gives one power and influence.
I don't have access to many people like he has, after all he is a scion of a rich family. Money talks, you know.

726. More haste, less speed.

When you try to do things too quickly you work less efficiently and ultimately take longer.

727. Move heaven and earth.

Make supreme effort
I'll move heaven and earth to finish in top 10 percentile in the exam.

728. Mufti .

An old army term for your non-military clothing. Used in schools for non-uniform days i.e Mufti-days

729. Mug .

A naïve or gullible person.

730. Na .

No.

731. Nail in someone's coffin.

Nail in someone's coffin is something that hastens failure of a person or thing
The scandal proved to be the final nail in the coffin of the mayor.

732. Necessity is the mother of invention.

A need or problem forces people to come up with innovative solutions.
In some parts of the world, farmers use washing machine to clean potatoes in large volumes. Necessity, after all, is the mother of invention.

733. Never look a gift horse in the mouth.

If someone offers you a gift, don't question it.

734. Never put off until tomorrow what you can do today.

Don't delay doing something if you can do it immediately.
I'm done with most of my assignment, but I'll pick the remaining part on Monday. Why don't you complete it now?

You'll be more relieved and in a better state of mind. You shouldn't put off until tomorrow what you can do today.

735. Nicked.

Commonly used as alternative to 'stolen'. Before more strict legislation, it was used by police as a term for arresting someone; 'you're nicked!'

736. No gain without pain.

It is necessary to suffer or work hard in order to succeed or make progress.
You've to drastically reduce the time you spend on video games and TV if you want to get admission in a good college. No gain without pain.

737. No man is an island.

You can't live completely independently. Everyone needs help from other people.

738. No news is good news.

If you don't receive any news about someone or something, it means that everything is fine and going normally.
My daughter has been working in Australia for nearly five years now. At first I used to get worried when I didn't hear from her, but now I know that no news is good news.

739. No smoke without fire.

A suspicion or rumor is not for nothing. It usually has some basis.
Example: I'm hearing that the investment company in which I put my money has been running a Ponzi scheme. I'm going to ask for my money back, because where there is smoke there is fire.

740. No strings attached.

Free of conditions
World Bank rarely gives loans with no strings attached.

741. Not the only fish in the sea.

Not the only suitable thing or person one can find
You shouldn't be so heartbroken at the rejection by her.
Remember, she's not the only fish in the sea.

742. Not your cup of tea.

If you say that someone or something is not your cup of
tea, you mean that they're not the kind of person or thing
you like.
Sales is not my cup of tea.

743. Nuts .

Crazy in a good or bad sense, particularly used as a
positive term amongst younger generations

744. On about .

As part of 'what are you on about?', 'on' replacing
'talking'.

745. On cloud nine.

If you're on cloud nine, you're very happy.
I was on cloud nine after receiving the news of my promotion.

746. On the ropes.

If someone is on the ropes, they're close to defeat or giving
up.
High crude oil prices have put many airlines on the ropes.

747. On thin ice.

If you're on thin ice, you're in precarious or delicate
situation.

You're falling short on class attendance and you failed to submit the last assignment. You're walking on thin ice in this semester.

748. On top of the world.

Extremely happy
I was on top of the world after landing the job I so badly wanted.

749. Once bitten twice shy.

You say this proverb when someone won't do something a second time because they had bad experience the first time.
I won't try this drink, because last time I had a burning sensation in my throat. Once bitten twice shy, I guess.

750. Once in a blue moon.

If something happens once in a blue moon, it happens rarely.
Many startups turn in a profit once in a blue moon.

751. One man's trash is another man's treasure.

Different people have different ideas about what's valuable.

752. One off .

A one time event.

753. One shouldn't miss forest for the trees.

Sometimes you get so focused on small details that you may miss the larger context.
The marketers got so bogged down on creating the perfect ad campaign that they didn't realize that the medium – Facebook – they wanted to use was no longer a viable option because of its recent algorithm updates.

754. Opposites attract..

People and things that seem to be diametrically opposed are often found to have a point of contact.

755. Out of sight, out of mind.

If someone or something is not seen for a long time, it'll be forgotten.
Many celebrities find a way to appear in media because they know that out of sight is out of mind.

756. Over my dead body.

If you say something will happen your dead body, you mean you dislike it and will do everything you can to prevent it.
We're selling your old bike to remove the junk that's gathering in the house. Over my dead body.

757. Paddle your own canoe.

Be independent and not need help from anyone.
After I went to boarding school in my teens, I started paddling my own canoe to a large extent.

758. Pants.

The Brits say 'trousers' ... The American default word for the article of clothing that covers the legs and pelvic region seems pretty general and innocuous to English speakers in the U.S.To the actual English, however, 'pants' is the primary word they use for 'underwear.' American cinema and television typically writes the word 'knickers' for underwear into the vocabulary of British characters *that's probably just for comedic effect since 'pants' wouldn't induce any response*

759. Pass the buck.

To deflect responsibility onto someone else.

760. Pay through the nose.

If you pay through the nose, you pay too much for something.
We're paying through the nose for petrol and diesel.

761. Pay someone back in his /her own coin.

If you pay someone back in his/ her own coin, you treat him/ her in the same way he/ she treated you.
By refusing to help her colleague, she paid him back in the same coin.

762. Pen is mightier than sword.

Thinking and writing have more influence on people and events than use of force.
After the mass killings at the newspaper office, there is a protest which is happening in the city declaring support to the paper and proving that pen is mightier than sword.

763. People who live in glass houses should not throw stones.

Don't criticize someone if you're not perfect either; don't be a hyprocrite
"Why are you always bothering her about being addicted to her phone? You've been smoking for 20 years and haven't been able to give it up. People who live in glass houses should not throw stones."

764. Piece of cake.

A metaphor to describe something that is easy or effortless.

765. Pig out.

A metaphor for binge eating.

766. Pissed Off .

Angry

767. Pissed .

Drunk

768. Play your cards right.

To behave or work in a way that gives you an advantage or improves your odds of success.
You've to play your cards right to cross level 4 in this game.

769. Plead the fifth.

References the fifth amendment to the U.S. Constitution, which allows a witness in court to refuse questions on the grounds that they risk self-incrimination.

770. Point finger at.

If you point finger at someone, you say that s/he should be blamed
Why are you pointing finger at me? I'm not the only person responsible for the loss.

771. Posh .

High class, sophisticated.

772. Pour cold water on.

If you pour cold water on an idea or plan, you criticize it to the extent that people lose enthusiasm to pursue it.
The investors poured cold water on the plan to build another factory.

773. Pour out one's heart.

If you pour out your heart, you reveal your
thoughts or inner feelings.
*I poured my heart out to my colleague about the mismanagement
in the Company.*

774. Practice makes perfect.

Doing something over and over makes one better at it.
*You can't expect to master guitar in two months. You've to keep
at it for several months, as practice makes perfect.*

775. Practice what you preach.

Behave in the way that you encourage other people to
behave in.
*You keep telling us to go for a jog in the morning, but I wish you
would practice what you preach.*

776. Prat .

A stupid, or badly behaved person.

777. Prejudice is the daughter of ignorance..

People often despise others about whom they only have
incomplete knowledge

778. Puke .

Vomit.

779. Pukka .

Originally describing genuine brands, now generally used
as 'excellent'

780. Put someone in his/ her place.

If you put people in their place, you let them know that
they're less important than they think.

When he exceeded his brief to take charge of the project, the boss put him in his place.

781. Put something to sleep.

If an animal is put to sleep, it is killed by a veterinarian to relieve it of its pain and suffering.
We put the dog to sleep as it was suffering from age-related ailments.

782. Put the cat among the pigeons.

If you put the cat among the pigeons, you say or do something that makes lot of people angry or uncomfortable.
She put the cat among the pigeons by accusing others in the office of misusing organization's dinner allowance for working late hours.

783. Put to bed.

To help a child sleep
Example:

784. Quid pro quo.

a favor or advantage granted or expected in return for something.
the pardon was a quid pro quo for their help in releasing hostages'

785. Quid .

One GBP (Great British Pound).

786. Raining cats and dogs.

If it rains cats and dogs, it rains heavily.
It has been raining cats and dogs for the last hour or so. Let's brace up for the traffic jam.

787. Rank .

Disgusting, revolting.

788. Read between the lines.

If you read between the lines, you try to understand someone's real feelings or intentions from what they say or write.
The government says that the economy is robust, but if you look at employment data and read further between the lines, you realize that the situation isn't that rosy.

789. Red sky at night shepherd's delight; red sky in the morning, shepherd's warning.

A red sunset signals nice weather ahead.

790. Ride Shotgun.

Another phrase taken from Old-West folklore, riding shotgun is a statement of both position and status
a sort of second-in-command support position who works from a preferential vantage.The imagery invoked by the phrase comes from stagecoaches, specifically the person who rode in the seat next to the driver whose job was to fend off any would-be bandits with a shotgun.

791. Right off the bat.

If you do something right off the bat, you do it immediately.
I learnt right off the bat that I need to build good rapport with the marketing team to do well in the organization.

792. Rome wasn't built in a day.

Important work takes time to complete.
You can't expect her to finish such a complex project in a week. Rome wasn't built in a day.

793. Rub salt into someone's wounds.

To make a bad thing worse
I was upset at not getting promoted, but the management really rubbed salt into my wounds when they promoted my junior.

794. Run around in circles.

To be active without achieving any worthwhile result
He ran around in circles trying to bring us on board for the new cause.

795. Run its course.

If something runs its course, it continues naturally until it f inishes.
There is no cure for this infection. You'll have to let it run its course.

796. Save your skin.

If you save your skin, you save yourself from an unpleasant or dangerous situation without thinking of what happens to others.
They lied and tampered with crucial evidence to save their skin.

797. Score .

20, often 20 GBP (Great British Pound).

798. Scrape the barrel.

When you're scraping the barrel, you're using something you do not want to but you've no option.
I was scraping the barrel when I had to stay for six months with my parents after I lost my job.

799. Screw up.

To make a mistake, i.e. Mess up.

800. See the light of day.

When something sees the light of day, it finally happens for the first time.
After so many false starts, his book finally saw the light of the day.

801. Sell like hot cakes.

If something sells like hot cakes, it sells very fast.
More than five thousand cars sold so far. The new model is selling like hot cakes.

802. Separate the wheat from the chaff.

If you separate wheat from the chaff, you separate valuable from worthless.
The new testing procedure to evaluate employees will separate the wheat from the chaff.

803. Set a beggar on horseback, and he'll ride to the devil..

People who suddenly acquire wealth or power are likely to misuse it.

804. Set in stone.

If something is set in stone, it's very difficult to change.
The contract isn't set in stone. If the deal is compelling enough, we're open to change it.

805. Set the record straight.

If you set the record straight, you quash misinformation about something by telling the truth.
Let me set the record straight on all the talk in the media about my business relationship with the key accused in the scandal.

806. She drives like a bat out of hell .

Presumably, a bat living in a deep cave which turns out to be an entrance to Hell would fly in a swift and crazy manner trying to get away. 'Her' driving would be just as crazed and frenetic.)

807. Shoot from the hip.

To speak bluntly or rashly without thinking carefully
If you want to be a spokesperson, you need to avoid your habit of shooting from the hip.

808. Shoot oneself in the foot.

To harm one's own cause inadvertently
He shot himself in the foot in the interview by disclosing too much personal information.

809. Shoot the breeze.

An idiomatic phrase for killing time with idle chit-chat, 'shoot the breeze probably stems from old-west imagery, either cinematic or anecdotal in origin, in which men with nothing but time and ammunition on their hands shot their guns at no particular target.

810. Show me a liar and i will show you a thief.

People who lie are even less trustworthy than people who thieve.

811. Show someone the door.

To ask someone to leave
During my worst period, I was promptly shown the door by very same people who once courted me.

812. Shut one's eyes to.

Refuse to see or consider
The government can no longer shut its eye to growing pollution arising from stubble burning.

813. Silence is half consent.

If you don't object to what someone says or does, you may be assumed to agree to some extent.
He didn't say anything to my proposal of going for a picnic on the weekend. I believe he is not saying 'no'. Silence is half consent.

814. Slow and steady wins the race.

Slow and consistent work leads to better chance of success than quick work in spurts.
I've built a strong vocabulary by learning a word a day for the last three years. Mine has been much less even though I've had days when I polished ten words. I guess slow and steady wins the race.

815. Small cog in a large wheel.

Someone or something that has a small role in a large setup or organization.
I work as a sales representative in a Fortune 500 company – just a small cog in a large wheel.

816. Smart .

Smart means clever and intelligent, but can be used derogatorily with sarcasm to undermine someone, such as 'don't get smart with me'

817. Smashing .

Positive exclamation, really good.

818. Snog .

Heavy kissing, like a french kiss.

819. Spill the Beans.

an American idiom for divulging secret information that dates back to the very early 1900s.
Someone for sure spilled the beans about the plan of jail inmates to smuggle in weapons. How else could jail authorities know about it?

820. Spoil someone's plans.

To ruin someone's plans
The heavy overnight rain spoilt our plan to play cricket next morning.

821. Spread yourself thin.

To try to do too many things at the same time, implying inadequate time or attention to any of them
College students, especially in first year, spread themselves thin by joining multiple elective courses and social activities.

822. Stab someone in the back.

Harm someone who trusts you.
It's not uncommon for people to stab colleagues in the back to move ahead in the professional world.

823. Start with a clean slate.

Make a fresh beginning forgetting what happened, usually bad, in the past
Example: Relations have not been great between the two countries, but it's time to start from a clean slate.

824. Stay the course.

If you stay the course, you persevere till the completion of a task, especially a difficult one.
Despite an injury, he stayed the course to save the match for his team.

825. Steal the show.

If you steal the show, you get lot of attention or credit in an event or show.
Chinese participants stole the show on the first day of 2018 Asian Games.

826. Stick to your guns.

If you stick to your guns in the face of opposition, you stand firm.
Despite opposition from his family, he has stuck to his guns in picking his career path.

827. Sticks and stones may break my bones,but words will never hurt me..

Adverse criticism or verbal abuse may be unpleasant, but it does no physical harm.

828. Stiff Upper Lip .

Not slang, but a very British phrase and characteristic of British people, describing fortitude in the face of adversity and great self restraint in the expression of emotion.

829. Still waters run deep.

If a person doesn't speak much, it doesn't mean they lack depth or are uninteresting.
She is one of the smartest persons in the organization. She may not talk much, but still waters run deep.

830. Stir up a hornets' nest.

Provoke trouble
It's not that the management is not aware of few false bills here and there, but they don't call it because it would expose many and stir up a hornet's nest.

831. Strike while the iron is hot.

Take advantage of an opportunity as soon as it exists.
I thought over the job offer I got way too long. Now it has been offered to someone else. I should have struck while the iron was hot.

832. Stupid is as stupid does.

an intelligent person who does stupid things is still stupid. You are what you do.

833. Swallow your pride.

If you swallow your pride, you do something even though it hurts your self-respect.
I swallowed my pride to do menial tasks for six months till I found a better job.

834. Sweet.

An adjective that describes something that is good, or nice.

835. Ta .

Casual thank you.

836. Take a back seat.

If you take a back seat, you choose not to be in a position of responsibility or power.
After being in the leadership position for more than a decade, it'll be tough for him to take a back seat.

837. Take a Rain Check .

Something you say when you cannot accept someone's invitation to do something but you would like to do it at another time.

838. Take away your breath.

If someone or something takes your breath away, it
astonishes you.
*His diving catch at the crunch moment in the match took my
breath away.*

**839.Take care of the pennies and the dollars will take care of
themselves..**

It is possible to become rich by making small profits.

840.Take somebody for a ride.

If you take somebody for a ride, you deceive them.
*The placement agency took hundreds of people for a ride by
promising non-existent jobs.*

841.Take the word out of somebody's mouth.

To say exactly what the other person was about to say
*Why don't we leave early today to watch the 5 PM show of the
latest release? You've taken the words out of my mouth. I was
about to say the same.*

842.Take with a Grain of Salt .

To consider something to not be completely true or right.

843.Taking the Piss/Mickey/Michael/Mick .

Mocking someone or thing, joking at someone or
somethings expense

844.Tenner .

10 GBP (Great British Pound).

845.Test waters.

If you test waters, you try to find how people will receive
your idea or action before actually launching it or telling
people.

The Company is testing waters with few products before going full steam.

846.That's fire! .

> This is the up-t0-the-minute version of the teenager slang for 'That is really amazing!' Older versions include cool, rad, swift, sick, awesome, cherry and 'on fleek'.)

847.The age of miracles is past.

> Miracles no longer happen; used when some desirable occurrence seems highly unlikely.

848.The appetite grows on what it feeds on..

> Desire or enthusiasm for something often increases as you do it

849.The apple never falls far from the tree.

> Children resemble their parents in character and nature.

850.The best art conceals art.

> Artistic excellence lies in making something that is subtle or intricate in construction appear simple and streamlined.

851.The best is the enemy of the good.

> By constantly striving for the best we risk destroying, or failing to produce, something good.

852.The best of men are but men at best.

> Even the greatest people have their failings and limitations.

853.The best things come in small packages.

Size has no bearing on quality, and a small container may hold something of great value; often said by or to a short person.

854. The best things in life are free.

The most rewarding or satisfying experiences in life are often those that cost nothing;also used of the wonders of nature or of abstract qualities such as health and friendship.

855. The best-laid plans go astray.

Despite best preparations, things may not go your way. *I had everything covered for this project, but now I'm told that the project can't go ahead because the Company is planning an organizational restructuring. Well, that's unfortunate, but sometimes the best-laid plans go astray.*

856. The biter is sometimes bit .

Those who criticize or otherwise set about others are not immune from criticism or other attack themselves.

857. The busiest men have the most leisure.

People who are industrious by nature always seem to have the most spare time,either because they accomplish their work more quickly and efficiently or because they cram so much into their busy lives.

858. The cat would eat fish, but would not wet her feet.

You must be prepared to put up with personal inconvenience, discomfort,or risk in order to get what you want;often used when somebody is hesitant about doing something for this reason.

859. The child is father of the man.

A child's character is an indication of the type of adult he or she will become — human nature does not change from youth to maturity.

860.The clock goes as it pleases the clerk.

It is up to civil servants and other bureaucrats how time is governed and spent.

861.The cold shoulder.

A metaphor for deliberately ignoring someone.

862.The company makes the feast.

You will enjoy a meal or celebration far more if you are among cheerful friendly people,and the quality of the food and drink — or of the surroundings — is of lesser importance.

863.The cowl does not make the monk.

Do not judge a person's character by his or her outward appearance or behavior.

864.The Daily Grind .

Someone's everyday work routine.

865.The danger past and God forgotten.

People are prone to calling on God in times of trouble, only to forget all about their newly found religious faith as soon as the crisis is past.

866.The devil dances in an empty pocket .

The poor are easily tempted to do evil.

867.The devil finds work for idle hands to do.

Idle people may find themselves tempted into wrongdoing.

868.**The devil is not as black as he is painted.**

People are rarely as bad as others say they are; often used in defense of a specific person.

869.**The devil looks after his own.**

Bad or undeserving people often prosper and thrive; said in response to the success or good fortune of such a person.

870.**The devil was sick, the devil a saint would be; the devil was well, the devil a saint was he.**

People often turn to religion or promise to reform when they are ill or in trouble, only to revert to their former ways as soon as the crisis is over.

871.**The devil's children have the devil's luck.Bad people often have good luck;usually said with envy rather than malice on hearing of somebody's good fortune.**

Bad or undeserving people often prosper and thrive; said in response to the success or good fortune of such a person.

872.**The difficult is done at once, the impossible takes a little longer.**

Difficult tasks present no problem, and even those that seem impossible will ultimately be accomplished; used as a motto or policy statement, as in commerce.

873.**The dog always returns to his vomit.**

People always return to the scene of their crime or wrongdoing.

874. **The early bird catches the worm.**

You should wake up and start work early if you want to succeed.

875. **The early bird gets the worm.**

People who wake up early or who get to places early have a better chance of success
"I got to the ticket office before anyone else. I got front row seats to the show! The early bird gets the worm."

876. **The end justifies the means.**

A desired result is so important that any method, even a morally bad one, may be used to achieve it.
He's campaigning with illegal funds on the theory that if he wins the election the end will justify the means.

877. **The enemy of my enemy is my friend.**

If someone whom I don't like doesn't like someone else whom I don't like, we can act like friends and unite against the other person (common in war)
"I don't like you, you don't like me. But I think we can agree that we both HATE Daniel. Let's work together and get him fired! The enemy of my enemy is my friend, right?"

878. **The exception proves the rule.**

The existence of an exception to a rule shows that the rule itself exists and is applicable in other cases; often used loosely to explain away any such inconsistency.

879. **The female of the species is deadlier than the male.**

Women often prove to be more dangerous than men, when roused to anger.

880.**The first hundred years are the hardest.**

Life will always be difficult; said jocularly or ironically to those who complain about their problems, sometimes with the implication that things will improve eventually.

881.**The game is not worth the candle.**

It is not worth persisting in an enterprise that is unlikely to yield enough profit or benefit to compensate for the effort or expense involved, or that carries a risk, actual harm or loss.

882.**The gods send nuts to those who have no teeth.**

Opportunities or good fortune often come too late in life for people to enjoy them or take full advantage of them; also applied more generally to people of any age who are unable to use or benefit from good things that come their way.

883.**The golden age was never the present age.**

The past and the future always seem infinitely preferable to the present time.

884.**The grass is always greener on the other side of the fence..**

People always want what they don't have
A: *"I'm jealous of all the free time my single friends have."*

885.**The gray mare is the better horse.**

A woman is often more competent or powerful than a man; used specifically of wives who have the upper hand over their husbands.

886.**The greater the truth, the greater the libel.**

Some people will take greater offense at a true accusation of wrongdoing than at a false one.

887.The hand that rocks the cradle rules the world.

Mothers have a powerful influence— if indirectly—on world affairs,because it is they who mold the characters of future leaders.

888.The harder you work, the luckier you get.

The harder you work, the more good ideas and chances you may make for yourself.
Many think he got lucky in getting that fat contract, but few know he had been pursuing dozens of such contracts for several weeks – the harder you work, the luckier you get.

889.The higher the monkey climbs the more he shows his tail.

People's faults and shortcomings become increasingly obvious as they advance to positions of high office.

890.The highest branch is not the safest roost.

Those in the highest positions of power or authority are, in some respects, the most vulnerable, because there will always be plenty of others eager to take their place or cause their downfall.

891.The hole calls the thief.

Criminals and other wrong-doers will go where opportunity presents itself.

892.The house shows the owner.

A person's character is revealed by the state of his or her house.

893.The king can do no wrong.

People in authority are not bound by the rules and regulations that apply to others; specifically, a monarch is above the law.

894. The laborer is worthy of his hire.

Those who work for others are entitled to be paid for their efforts.
Bible Reference: Luke 10:7

895. The last drop makes the cup run over.

One final additional thing may push a person beyond his or her limit of tolerance or endurance.

896. The last straw (or the straw that broke the camel's back).

If an event is the last straw, it is the last in a series of unpleasant or undesirable events that exceeds your limit of tolerance.
Recent hikes in fuel prices are the last straw for the lower middle class.

897. The lion is not so fierce as he is painted.

Some people have reputations that far exceed their real characters.

898. The longest way around is the shortest way home.

It is best to do things carefully and thoroughly rather than trying to cut corners.

899. The luck of the devil.

If you've the luck of the devil, you're extremely lucky.
I'm alive today because I failed to board the plane that crashed yesterday. You really have the luck of the devil.

900. The man who is born in a stable is not a horse. .

A person does not necessarily have the stereotypical characteristics of the place where he or she was born.

901.The meek shall inherit the earth. .

Humility will ultimately be rewarded.

902.The mills of God grind slowly, yet they grind exceedingly small. .

Retribution may be a long time in coming, but it cannot be avoided; also loosely applied to any slow or painstaking process

903.The other side of the coin.

The other point of view
We only see the glamor and money in showbiz. But the other side of the coin is that only one in hundreds reach there.

904.The pen is mightier than the sword.

If you're trying to convince someone of something, words and ideas are stronger than using physical force (common in politics)
"We must avoid this war and use diplomacy to solve our problems.The pen is mightier than the sword."

905.The post of honor is the post of danger; uneasy lies the head that wears a crown..

Those in the highest positions of power or authority are, in some respects, the most vulnerable, because there will always be plenty of others eager to take their place or cause their downfall.

906.The pot calling the kettle black.

Accusing someone of faults that you yourself have
He called me a cheat – that's pot calling the kettle black.

907.**The pot is calling the kettle black.**

People should not criticize someone else for a fault that
they themselves have.
*He accused me of being selfish. Talk about the pot calling the
kettle black!*

908.**The proof of the pudding is in the eating.**

You can only judge the quality of something after you
have tried, used, or experienced it.
*Marketers have claimed that this weight loss diet produces
strong results in just two months. Well, I'll reserve my opinion
till I've tried it myself. After all, proof of pudding is in the
eating.*

909.**The road to hell is paved with good intentions.**

Good intentions do not matter if a person's actions lead to
bad outcomes.
*Well, I was only trying to be helpful by mixing those two acids.
But, it exploded the beaker. Well, the road to hell is paved with
good intentions.*

910.**The show must go on.**

A performance, event, etc., must continue even though
there are problems.
The chairman died yesterday but the show must go on.

911.**The squeaky wheel gets the grease.**

The person who complains in a situation is more likely to
get something.
*A: "I just don't understand why she's received so many
promotions, and I'm still at the bottom of the company!"*

912.**The tail is wagging the dog.**

If the tail is wagging the dog, then a small or unimportant part of something is becoming too important and is controlling the whole thing.
Their group is small but very vocal, so be sure that management doesn't give in to their demands. We don't want the tail wagging the dog, after all.

913.The tongue is not steel, but it cuts..

Words can hurt deeply.

914.There are more ways of killing a cat than choking it with cream..

There are many different ways to achieve the same result,or to come to the same conclusion

915.There are more ways than one to skin a cat.

There is more than one way to reach the same goal.
We can get around that by renting instead of buying the delivery van – there's more than one way to skin a cat.

916.There is no place like home.

Your home is the most comfortable place in the world
"What a tiring vacation! I'm glad to be back in my own bed again.There's no place like home."

917.There is no such thing as a free lunch..

Nothing is free. Even the things that are free have a hidden cost
"His bank gave him $50 for free, but he had to commit to opening a credit card account.There's no such thing as a free lunch."

918.There is no time like the present.

The best time to do something is right now. So, act now. *Don't wait until New Year to change this bad habit. There's no time like the present.*

919. There is safety in numbers.

A group offers more protection than when you are on your own.
Her parents won't allow her to date but do let her go to parties, saying there's safety in numbers.

920. There's more than one way to skin a cat.

There are many different ways to achieve the same result, or to come to the same conclusion

921. There's no fool like an old fool..

People who have not gained the wisdom of experience by the time they reach middle age are likely to remain fools for the rest of their lives

922. There's no smoke without fire; what everybody says must be true..

Rumors are rarely without substance, and if unpleasant things are being said about somebody, then that person has probably done something to deserve them.

923. There's no such thing as a free lunch.

Things that are offered for free always have a hidden cost.

924. There's no time like the present.

If you need to do something, don't wait until later. Do it now.

925. There's nowt so queer as folk.

Nothing is as strange as people can be; people can behave very oddly sometime

926.They that live longest see most..

Do not presume to give advice or instruction to those who are older and more experienced than you.

927.Thorn in your flesh.

A person or thing that continually irritates or troubles you
Demanding coalition partners have been a thorn in the flesh of the government.

928.Through thick and thin.

If you do something through thick and thin, you do it whether circumstances are good or not.
He is one of those rare employees who has remained with the organization through thick and thin.

929.Throw a spanner in the work.

To disrupt or cause problems in an activity or project
Last-minute withdrawal of the sponsor threw a spanner in our plans to organize the cultural festival.

930.Throw caution to the wind.

Behave or speak in a rash manner
Just to impress others, he threw caution to the wind and climbed the steep rock without any safety gear.

931.Throw one's weight around.

To act in a way that suggests you've lot of power or authority
The politician tried to throw his weight around with the police, but the police ignored him.

932. Throw up one's hands.

To express anger or frustration when a situation becomes unacceptably bad
The manager threw up his hands in despair when nothing concrete emerged even after hours of negotiations.

933. Tight.

An adjective that describes closeness between competitors, i.e. A tight competition.

934. Time and tide wait for no man.

You've no control over passage of time; it'll keep slipping. So don't procrastinate, don't delay things.
We need to hurry up or else we'll miss the flight. Time and tide wait for no man.

935. To come to a head.

If something comes to a head, it reaches to the point of a crisis.
The situation came to a head when he passed a derogatory comment purportedly toward me.

936. To Each his Own .

One has a right to one's personal preferences.

937. To know which side your bread is buttered on.

Be aware of where one's best interests lie.
I know which side my bread is buttered on. So, I was very nice to the recruiter and promptly sent her a thank you card after our interview.

938. Toe the line.

If you toe the line, you behave according to an official rule, especially when you do not agree with it.
In this organization, if you don't toe the line, you'll be fast eased out.

939.Too many cooks spoil the broth.

When too many people work together on a project, the result is inferior.
This proposal has received feedback from too many parliamentary committees, and that's probably the reason why it lacks clear actionables. I've no doubt that too many cooks spoil the broth.

940.Trash.

Can be used as an intransitive verb for destruction. E.g. "He trashed the car."

941.Trust not one night's ice..

Before relying upon something (or someone), it is best to test it first.

942.Try one's patience.

To test the limit of one's patience
The constant chatter at the back of the class tried the professor's patience.

943.Turn a deaf ear.

If you turn a deaf ear, you ignore what others are saying.
I've made the request few times in the past, but it has always fallen on deaf ears.

944.Turn the clock back.

If you turn the clock back to an earlier period, you return to that time.
Turning the clock back to our glory days is fruitless. We've to work harder and smarter in the present.

945.Turn the tables on somebody.

To completely reverse circumstances or gain upper hand
on someone who was previously in a stronger position.
*He turned the tables on his political opponent by reeling off data
on how poorly the economy has fared in the last one year.*

946.Turn the tide.

To reverse the course of events from one extreme to
another
*With that goal right at the start of the second half, the home team
seems to be turning the tide against their arch rivals.*

947.Twat .

Harsh insult but not quite swearing, more extreme than
'Prat'.

948.Twist someone's arm.

Make someone do something by pressurizing them
*The government brought the rebel leaders to the negotiating
table by twisting their arms by launching investigation into
their shady business deals.*

949.Two heads are better than one.

It's easier to do something as a team than by yourself
*"I'm stuck on this project. Can you help me out? Two heads are
better than one."*

950.Two wrongs don't make a right.

You shouldn't harm a person who has harmed you, even if
you think that person deserves it.
*Just because he insulted you doesn't mean it's OK for you to
start a rumor about him – two wrongs don't make a right.*

951. Under a cloud.

If you're under a cloud, you're under suspicion or in trouble.
The IP for our key technology has been leaked, and many in my team, including the manager, are under a cloud.

952. Under someone's nose.

If you do something under someone's nose, you do it openly, although unnoticed.
The dog took away the biscuit right under my nose, but I realized it only later.

953. Uni .

short word for university.

954. Up for it .

Very willing to do something.

955. Up in arms.

Angry about something
Media has traditionally been up in arms with the government of the day.

956. Upset someone's applecart.

If you upset someone's applecart, you do something that causes a plan to go wrong.
The increase in customs duty by the government has upset the applecart of those car companies who were importing most of their car parts.

957. Uptight.

Stuffy, persnickety, the opposite of relaxed.

958. Virtue is its own reward.

You should not be virtuous in hopes of getting a reward, but because it makes you feel good to be virtuous.

959. Wake up on the Wrong Side of the Bed .

To feel grumpy; irritable; to be easily annoyed.

960. Walk a tightrope.

If you walk a tightrope, you do something that allows little room for error.
Many educational institutions have to walk a tightrope between charging a high tuition fee and facing criticism, and not charging much and depending on grants.

961. Wash dirty linen in public.

If you wash your dirty linen in public, you discuss those matters in public which should have been kept private.
The two brothers went public accusing each other of fraud, washing dirty linen in the public in the process.

962. Watch one's step.

Be careful about how you behave or conduct yourself, lest you get into trouble
Watch your steps at least in the first few months at your new job.

963. Wealth makes many friends..

Wealthy people never lack friends — or those who claim to be their friends until their money runs out.

964. Wear two/ several hats.

To function in more than one capacity
He wears two hats in the company – Chief Marketing Officer and Chief Information Officer.

965. Wear your heart on your sleeve.

If you wear your heart on your sleeve, you express your sentiments too openly.
Wearing your heart on your sleeve can backfire at workplace because you may be seen unprofessional.

966. What goes around comes around.

If someone treats other people badly, he or she will eventually be treated badly by someone else.
He tormented me back in high school, and now he has his own bully. What goes around comes around.

967. What the eye doesn't see, the heart doesn't grieve over..

People often admire others about whom they only have incomplete knowledge

968. When in Rome, do as the Romans do.

When visiting a foreign land, follow the customs of local people.
I don't love cotton candy, but we are at a carnival. When in Rome, do as the Romans do, right?

969. When push comes to shove.

When situation turns desperate
If push comes to shove, I'll take loan to finance my education.

970. When the going gets tough, the tough get going.

When conditions become difficult, strong people take action.
I know you're not used to climbing at such heights, but come on when the going gets tough, the tough get going.

971. When the oak is before the ash, then you will only get a splash; when the ash is before the oak, then you may expect a soak.

A traditional way of predicting whether the summer will be wet or dry on the basis of whether the oak leaves appear first.

972. Where one door shuts, another opens.

When you lose an opportunity to do one thing, an opportunity to do something else appears.
I failed to get into my dream college. Don't worry, this has happened to many. I'm sure something better is waiting for you. Where one door shuts, another opens.

973. Where there's a will, there's a way.

If you are determined enough, you can find a way to achieve what you want, even if it is very difficult.
He had little resources to start his business, but he eventually did through a small opening – blog. Where there's a will, there's a way.

974. Where there's smoke there's fire.

If there are rumors or signs that something is true so it must be at least partly true.
Do you believe those rumors about the mayor? Well, you know what they say, where there's smoke, there's fire.

975. Where there's muck there's brass.

There is money to be made in unpleasant dirty jobs.

976. While the cat's away, the mice will play.

Without supervision, people will do as they please, especially in disregarding or breaking rules.

As soon as their parents left, the children invited all their friends over – when the cat's away, you know.

977. White elephant.

Something that is white elephant costs a lot (on maintenance etc.) to keep, but does little useful
The new Formula 1 race track is proving to be a white elephant for the owners. It is used for just few weeks in the year, but sucks a lot in maintenance.

978. Whose bread i eat, his song i sing..

The person who pays for a service or finances a project has the right to say how it should be done.

979. Wicked .

Formally meaning bad, but in slang meaning cool or exciting.

980. Wild-goose chase.

A search that turns out to be time-wasting and unsuccessful because the thing being searched doesn't exist or you were given wrong information about its location
The treasure hunt to find gold coins expectedly proved to be a wild-goose chase.

981. Wind up .

A situation that is very annoying.

982. Wonders will never cease!.

New unbelievable things occur.

983. Worth its weight in gold.

If someone or something is worth its weight in gold, they're of high value.
The new hire is worth her weight in gold. She has helped us land three big deals this quarter.

984. Wrap (something) up.

To finish or complete something.

985. You ain't just whistlin' Dixie. .

You are serious; you aren't playing around. This originates from the idea that the states which seceded from the Union during the USA's Civil War weren't thought to be really serious at first. 'Dixie' was the unofficial anthem of the South.)

986. You can catch more flies with honey than with vinegar.

It's easier to win people to your side by persuasion and politeness than by confrontation and threats.
The courier service has taken more time to deliver than they had promised. I want to take the issue up with them and get a refund. I would suggest you deal with them politely. You can catch more flies with honey than with vinegar.

987. You can lead a horse to water but you can't make it drink.

You can show people the way to do things, but you can't force them to act.
He has received all the resources one needs to start a business, but even after six months I don't see anything happening. Well, you can lead a horse to water but you can't make it drink.

988. You can't always get what you want.

Sometimes you may face disappointments in your pursuits or your wishes may not be fulfilled.
I want a bike on my birthday. Sorry, you can't always get what you want.

989. You can't fit a round peg in a square hole.

You can't force someone into a role for which s/he is not suited.
It took me a while, but I eventually understood that I was a round peg in a square hole in the firm. That's why I quit for a better fitting role.

990. You can't have your cake and eat it too.

To have two things that one desires, but they're normally impossible to get simultaneously.
If you want more local services, you can't expect to pay less tax. Well, you can't have your cake and eat it.

991. You can't make an omelette without breaking eggs.

It is hard to achieve something important without causing unpleasant effects.
If I don't slash people's salaries, the company is going to go bankrupt. It's unfortunate, but you can't make an omelet without breaking eggs.

992. You can't perform with one arm tied behind your back.

If you've to work with one arm tied behind, you work with a big handicap.
How do you expect me to win that deal without the flexibility to reduce price? You can't expect me to deliver results with one arm tied behind my back.

993. You can't run with the hare and hunt with the hounds.

You can't support both sides of a conflict or dispute.
How can you be taken seriously as a reformer when you have continued to accept gifts? You can't run with the hare and hunt with the hounds, Senator.

994. You can't teach an old dog new tricks.

People who have long been used to doing things in a particular way will not abandon their habits.
I bet you can't get him to get up at 5 AM and go out for a walk. After all, you can't teach an old dog new tricks.

995. You can't win them all.

It is not possible to succeed at everything you do.
I know you're disappointed to not convert that interview, but you can't win them all.

996. You can't always get what you want.

Don't whine and complain if you don't get what you wanted.

997. You can't judge a book by its cover.

Things sometimes look different than they really are. A restaurant that looks old and small might have amazing food, for example.

998. You can't make an omelet without breaking a few eggs.

When you try to do something great, you'll probably make a few people annoyed or angry. Don't worry about those people; just focus on the good results.

999. You lie like a dog! .

Meaning you are as excellent at telling an untruth as a dog is who can 'lie' around and sleep all day; variant: you lie like a rug)

1000. You scratch my back and I'll scratch yours.

If you help me, I'll help you.
If you help me get customers, I'll put in a good word for you. You scratch my back and I'll scratch yours.

1001. You should know which way the wind is blowing.

Anticipate how a certain plan or situation will likely unfold.
I think I'll see which way the wind is blowing before I vote at the board meeting.

1002. You show me the man and I'll show you the rule.

Rules change depending on how influential or powerful the person likely to be affected by the rules is.
He has been treated leniently by the police. That's why they say – you show me the man and I'll show you the rule.

1003. Youth is wasted on the young.

The young fail to appreciate what they experience.

1004. Zonked.

Completely exhausted.Our next post will cover British slang terms that Americans find confusing. Until then, here are some of our favorite American slang words:

Topical Index

bribery   37
brothers   103, 961
busy   132, 222, 225, 225, 261,
713, 857
buying   118, 915
cake   80, 80, 478, 478, 990, 990
calm   118, 346
cannot   42, 55, 56, 63, 63, 116,
124, 128, 128, 249, 405, 492, 499,
541, 543, 549, 551, 571, 837, 902
capacity   76, 424, 512
carpenter   61
cats   104, 786, 786, 786
caught   105, 192, 192, 192, 226
cause   49, 221, 247, 335, 396,
473, 565, 642, 808, 890, 905, 929
change   18, 18, 63, 85, 140, 224,
240, 240, 529, 544, 544, 552, 555,
555, 601, 677, 804, 859, 918, 1002
character   23, 95, 174, 185, 196,
254, 459, 460, 613, 666, 849, 859,
863, 892
check   88, 589
choice   104, 709
circumstances 105, 135, 249, 249,
928, 945
clock   99, 99, 860, 944, 944, 944
cold   144, 209, 209, 260, 390,
390, 568, 568, 568, 645, 645, 772,
772, 772, 861
college   106, 547, 736, 972
comes   107, 108, 138, 248, 271,
410, 484, 486, 610, 724, 724, 790,
935, 966, 966, 969, 969
communication 113

company   98, 347, 365, 461, 694,
719, 739, 815, 862, 964, 991
competence   3
competitors   85, 933
consider   89, 842
costs   100, 126, 126, 977
course   86, 263, 502, 824, 824,
946
court   71, 100, 769
created   109
crisis   133, 228, 701, 865, 870
criticism   49, 382, 404, 428, 474,
496, 827, 856, 960
crops   24
cure   25, 795
dark   84
daughter   96, 738, 777
daylight   144, 287
deal   85, 160, 253, 374, 418, 582,
720, 804, 986, 992
defamation   49
degree   130, 678
demeanor   41
deputy   141
devil   149, 190, 190, 192, 192,
192, 364, 437, 449, 503, 866, 867,
868, 869, 870, 870, 870, 870, 899
difficulty   45, 321
disgrace   2
disputes   100, 328
distance   111,
divine   112, 447, 450
doctor   125, 125, 211
door   20, 61, 149, 253, 253, 253,
407, 407, 565, 811, 972, 972
doubt   95, 939

668, 718, 720, 720, 736, 738, 738,
743, 791, 834, 869, 871, 871, 871,
882, 882, 888, 909, 909, 928, 958,
998, 1000
goose   49, 313, 313, 313, 625,
625
gossip   22, 22, 458
government   118, 163, 214, 352,
426, 482, 788, 812, 948, 955, 956
graduate   106
grist   108
grow   83, 90, 90, 111, 144, 145,
566, 723, 723, 723
guitar   88, 774
hand   7, 295, 304, 304, 330, 467,
467, 707, 885, 887, 945
hang   113, 428, 431, 496
happy   53, 471, 471, 472, 472,
588
harbor   83, 83
hard   45, 121, 134, 222, 338,
338, 338, 338, 403, 446, 473, 474,
486, 486, 658, 736, 991
hardship   98, 719
harm   48, 49, 309, 400, 531, 587,
808, 881, 950
harvest   24
health   114, 191, 854
healthy   141, 191, 191
heart   90, 90, 481, 481, 481, 511,
511, 773, 773, 965, 965, 965, 967
help   88, 135, 407, 426, 446,
446, 485, 514, 514, 522, 638, 737,
757, 761, 783, 784, 949, 1000, 1000,
1000

home   57, 74, 93, 280, 525, 525,
525, 679, 706, 916, 946
honest   41, 527, 528
hope   134, 442, 490, 491, 530,
531, 532
horse   42, 55, 319, 349, 363, 411,
411, 427, 486, 550, 733, 987, 987
hospital   126, 191
hours   144, 261, 318, 495, 932
house   56, 57, 57, 57, 57, 58, 90,
177, 189, 221, 319, 756, 892
hugging   79
human   21, 447, 450, 532, 532
hurry   120, 484, 537, 537, 713,
934
husband   43, 43, 44, 189, 621
idea   115, 153, 441, 637, 772,
845, 985
ideas   113, 215, 215, 376, 751,
888, 904
idle   132, 132, 142, 408, 596,
809, 867
idleness   142
illegal   147, 492, 876
illuminate   58
image   79
immediately   85
impossible   112, 224, 245, 509, 509,
682, 872, 872, 990
industry   111
inferior   102, 109, 154, 420, 447,
608
infirmities   20
influence   28, 29, 37, 282, 762
injury   130, 824
insubordination   55

working   99, 134, 222, 467, 544, 570, 738, 782
workman   3
world   65, 455, 572, 732, 748, 887
worry   14, 159, 276, 307, 649, 662, 972, 998

wrong   130, 152, 152, 160, 160, 160, 160, 249, 310, 433, 582, 601, 980
wrongdoers   130, 298, 377
yesterday   129, 609, 899, 910
youth   52, 859

Made in the USA
Monee, IL
03 July 2021